T

Comfort
Delusion

Based on Sermons on the Gospel of Mark

TOM SHAW

with

LIZ JENNINGS

Cover design © 2019 Tiffany Aicklen and Jerrod Turner

ISBN: 1-9997464-3-0
ISBN-13: 978-1-9997464-3-8

For Josie; my brave and courageous wife
who again and again has chosen the comfort of Christ
over the comforts of this world.

CONTENTS

Welcome

My wife, Josie, has a very high pain threshold. She's given birth three times and never really complained about the pain during any of the labours. She recently fell while running and broke her jaw in two places: covered in blood and clearly shocked, she still made very little fuss about the horrendous situation she found herself in.

I, however, am a little different. Pain is not something I naturally deal well with. I'm not just talking about those extreme moments like breaking a bone or going through a physical ordeal. I mean pretty much any level of pain. Not just physical pain, either. In fact, emotional pain can be worse: the pain of disapproval; of not being in control; of not being the centre. Why does it all hurt so much?

I am a child of my time and so the god (small 'g') of comfort has been a big part of my life. I love comfort. I love my daily, comfortable routine of good quality coffee in my lovely house in a beautiful part of the world. I like time with people, but generally only people I'm comfortable with. I love to pray, but only for the length of time I'm comfortable with. I give money, but only the amount and frequency which I am comfortable with. The truth about my love of comfort is far from comfortable to face up to.

The trouble is, all this comfort is killing me. It's a liar, you see. It's the road to death. Comfort promises so much yet always, always, always leads to a hollow and soul destroying conclusion. It never results in a life that is deeply soul-satisfying nor powerful to our bones.

Comfort-worship is alive and well today, particularly in the West, promising so much but actually, secretly responsible for so much misery. We often see the symptoms but don't know the cause. We see the quiet boredom, the creeping sense of entitlement, the inability to be thankful; we feel painfully aware of the cancer of comparison, yet we don't know how to get free.

I have seen myself become a fragile prima-donna, needing everything to be perfect before I can feel ok. I can react with alarming emotion when the things I normally rely on to make my life comfortable are taken away.

I say and I sing, *'All I need is you, Jesus,'* but the fragility I display and the ferocity of my emotions demonstrates I'm actually an addict. An addict of the drug that promises a high and instead delivers death.

Now, I'm not saying comfort in itself is wrong: this is not a puritanical rant. My desire is for this book to draw you closer into God's comfort, because so many of our problems come when we pursue comfort in-and-of-itself, rather than as the side effect and natural overflow from the primary goal of a real relationship with Jesus Christ. Comfort itself is not 'wrong' to pursue, but if it is not found in Christ, it becomes a deadly trap we become ensnared in.

Are you prone to react more emotionally than you'd like when life

2

gets uncomfortable? I see it in my own life, even in small things: when the wrong delivery is made to my house; when the driver ahead drives slower than I want; when the supermarket doesn't have the item I'd hoped for. I see it in the bigger things, too: when colleagues are promoted and praised and not me; when illness strikes and requires embracing and enduring a season of pain and discomfort. Like I said, it's not comfortable facing up to comfort.

If any or all of the above resonates with you, then like me, probably there's some work to be done in weaning you off the deeply embedded expectation that *life should be comfortable*. And if you're a Christian, perhaps even the expectation that Jesus should make your life more comfortable.

The book in your hands flowed out of my own personal struggles with the god of comfort, and is based upon a series of sermons preached in 2012 at The City Church, in Canterbury, England. It was over a beer one night with my friend Mike Rayner that the idea for this book was suggested. He felt it fell somewhere between a themed book and a bible commentary, meaty and bible-based, but with the opportunity to roam around within a theme and explore it thoroughly. Liz Jennings, a gifted writer from our church family, was dropping some baby clothes at our house one evening when I shared Mike's suggestion with her. She agreed the sermon series had been an important one in terms of shaping her thinking too, and was enthusiastic about attempting to translate my spoken word into written form. It felt like perhaps God was in this. And so we took a step in faith, and *The Comfort Delusion* was born.

My view is that through the first half of the Gospel of Mark, Jesus is repeatedly inviting people to know Him and His love for them. But in this second half of Mark - chapters 9-16 - the cost and reality of following Jesus is made plain. It's a direct challenge to the love of comfort which must be acknowledged, repented of, and separated from. There can't be any halfway house or any attempt to be joined to both Christ *and* our previous love. Jesus is the lover of our soul. He alone now beckons us to trust Him. To put all our eggs in His basket, as it were. To step out of the boat of comfort and walk on the water in faith. To not be scared of leaving behind the broken, lying cesspit of comfort and bit by bit, breaking free to need Him and Him alone. It *is* possible. It *is* our destiny. It is *not* for a chosen few; not only for Christians who are being persecuted and whose life is unavoidably uncomfortable.

This is the path every Christian must take. It is not an option, it is the only way, I believe, by which we can truly follow Jesus. It is right there in the first commandment: 'You shall have no other gods before me.' (Exodus 20:3). That's a big ask, when so many other gods fight for our attention and worship. But we are not left alone to push through the pain. This is not a case of gritting our teeth and bearing it.

The heart of Jesus is more loving, assuring, equipping and empowering that we can fully grasp. As Dallas Willard put it: *'Yes the cost of discipleship is great. But the cost of un-discipleship even greater.'* He's right. The alternative to not doing this is allowing our lives to be swallowed by the deadly disease of pain-avoidance and sacrifice-resistance. Jesus, the Good Shepherd, wants to get glory through us fearful little sheep finding ourselves quietly, supernaturally empowered to spot and resist the old patterns of our hearts, minds and bodies.

He's not calling us to *be* heroes, but to *know* The Hero. Really. Truly. Deeply. In a way that will shock, amaze and thrill us. Knowing

4

Him in all his love, grace and mercy will empower us far more than we could have ever imagined in not needing those *things* – approval, possessions, status and so on – that we are constantly told we need.

It is my belief that if we are able to grow just even a little bit in this one area of discipleship, it would have a massive and lasting impact. It brings me back to something my wife, Josie, often says: God can do so much with so little.

This is the call to take a baby-step together. Not an overwhelming, utterly beyond us, unrealistic deal but, as we shall see, to take the hand of Jesus, and say 'Ok...you know how weak, fragile and unimpressive I am: lead me on today. Show me where comfort is holding me back, where risk avoidance has paralyzed me, where playing it safe has become my mantra, where I've become so set in my ways that I'm no longer led by the Spirit. Take me Jesus, fragile as I am, and sow something new in my life.'

In 2 Corinthians 1:3, Paul describes the 'God of all comfort.' Paul was a man who knew pain – physical, emotional and spiritual – but he discovered that every comfort he needed was to be found in the one true source.

May the God (big 'G') of all comfort meet you as you read, and may he bless you as you walk ever closer to him.

Tom Shaw, California, USA
August 2019

Chapter One

Mark 9: 14-29

From Mountain Top to Monday Morning

Picture the scene: Jesus, Peter, James and John are walking back down the mountainside together following Jesus' transfiguration. On that peak, Jesus physically changed before their eyes, was joined by two men long dead, and then God's voice boomed down from a cloud. Imagine the conversation they must have been having - can you hear Peter cringing as he reflects on his idea to build an altar at the top of the mountain? I can't believe I just said that! I'm so embarrassed! But I didn't know what else to say - that was mind-blowing!

And Jesus must have been beaming - don't you think? Grinning with the joy of having revealed something wonderful about himself to his closest friends, knowing that generations would read about what had just happened and be blessed by it.

So, in this frame of mind, the four of them arrive back at base camp, as it were, to be reunited with the other nine disciples. However, when they get there, the mood amongst their friends is far from cheerful.

Mark 9: 14 – 29

Jesus heals a boy with an unclean spirit

And when they came to the disciples, they saw a great crowd around them, and scribes arguing with them. And immediately all the crowd, when they saw him, were greatly amazed and ran up to him and greeted him. And he asked them, "What are you arguing about with them?" And someone from the crowd answered him, "Teacher, I brought my son to you, for he has a spirit that makes him mute. And whenever it seizes him, it throws him down, and he foams and grinds his teeth and becomes rigid. So I asked your disciples to cast it out, and they were not able." And he answered them, "O faithless generation, how long am I to be with you? How long am I to bear with you? Bring him to me." And they brought the boy to him. And when the spirit saw him, immediately it convulsed the boy, and he fell on the ground and rolled about, foaming at the mouth. And Jesus asked his father, "How long has this been happening to him?" And he said, "From childhood. And it has often cast him into fire and into water, to destroy him. But if you can do anything, have compassion on us and help us." And Jesus said to him, "If you can'! All things are possible for one who believes." Immediately the father of the child cried out and said, "I believe; help my unbelief!" And when Jesus saw that a crowd came running together, he rebuked the unclean spirit, saying to it, "You mute and deaf spirit, I command you, come out of him and never enter him again." And after crying out and convulsing him terribly, it came out, and the boy was like a corpse, so that most of

8

them said, "H .... *him up, and he arose. Ana* .... *m privately, "Why could n* .... *d cannot be driven out by a* ....

Talk about coming back down to earth with a bump! They return from the transfiguration to discover that their friends are in a mess, arguing with the increasingly angry crowd that surrounds them; a scene of hostile confusion reigns here. At the root of it all lies a lack of power on the disciples' behalf, and a failure to do the very things that Christianity claims to specialise in: healing in both the spiritual and physical realms.

Back in Mark 6, Jesus instructed the twelve disciples to cast out demons and heal the sick, and the gospel account tells us that they've been doing just that. Consequently, we can imagine that their reputation would have been growing. They've been healing people with all sorts of ailments, and feeding thousands from a single packed lunch... they've learnt from experience that Jesus is limitless in his capabilities.

They've been confidently proclaiming that God's Kingdom has come, and people are starting to approach them to find out what difference that can make to their own lives. But, in this critical moment, the disciples are suddenly lacking power, and are lost in the confusion of their experience.

How about you?

Have you ever felt afraid to pray for that colleague, friend or relative to be healed in case nothing happens?

Do you hesitate to make claims for Jesus that you may be asked to back up with a practical demonstration?

Does your fear of the potential anti-climax of prayer that is not instantly answered - like a magic spell with a missing ingredient - hold you back from praying bold prayers?

God is wanting to lovingly show us the reality of what we're called to here. Christianity is not about 'doing magic': it's about a deepening and authentic relationship with Christ, for each one of us.

No Lone Rangers

When we say that we know God, that he can heal us and change us, and he's risen from the dead, and that there's power right now to heal the sick and to see life transformation, we have to understand that those who are coming to us will inevitably say 'Okay then, let's see that happen.'

Perhaps you've had an experience just like the disciples of a complete anti-climax: hope extinguished, promises empty, power - gone. It leaves us crushed as believers, and does nothing to glorify the Father or proclaim his Kingdom.

So, what might we learn from the disciples painful experience?

Autopilot Alert

In Mark 9:17, we see a father who has brought his son to see the disciples. His son appears to have a medical problem (epilepsy) as well as a spiritual problem (he's demonised). The man knows who Jesus is, and he knows that he doesn't have to wait until Jesus comes back from the mountain top to secure healing for his son. He has approached the disciples directly, because he is aware of their reputation as healers.

But, when Jesus returns, this father turns to him with his complaint - in much the same way we might ask to see the manager of a shop if we had an issue with a member of staff.

'I asked your disciples to cast it out, and they were not able.' (v18b)

He's absolutely right to say this. In fact, he's providing us with a perfect definition of what it means to live a Christian life.

To live as a Christian and do and be all that it involves is not simply difficult: it's downright impossible!

God has allowed these disciples to suddenly taste their inability to do the supernatural things that He has called them to do.

In another of the gospels, Jesus sends a group of about seventy Christians out on mission, and he says *'...I am sending you out as lambs in the midst of wolves'* (Luke 10:3). You don't have to be David Attenborough to work out who would win in a fight between lambs and wolves. Jesus' definition of Christians doing what God has told them they should do is to be utterly vulnerable. To make it worse, he says *'Take nothing with you'* (verse 4). He's ramming it home that we are entirely dependent on God. He knows our tendency will be to think that we can survive on our wits and our finances, and he wants us to be acutely aware that we can't! Each one of us needs to stay 24/7 in a war with that part of our hearts that slips into the autopilot mode of self-sufficiency.

Now, I'm no pilot, but I get the idea that when a plane is at 35,000 feet in blue sky and everything's hunkydory, that's when you press the autopilot button. And I just wonder here whether perhaps these disciples are cruising on previous spiritual experiences and the reputation they've gained because of them. It's that old 'two years ago I had a really amazing quiet time' chestnut.

The Christian life is not like cruising at 35,000 feet. It's more like flying a plane through a mountain range! You don't stick autopilot on in a mountain range: you're alert at every moment, giving it every ounce of your attention.

The moment that autopilot attitude starts to set in in my life is the moment when it can all go wrong.

The disciples' weakness was in knowing that they were weak! They had slipped into a presumptuous, autopilot attitude - 'This is the sort of thing we can do - we've done it before,' blagging their way through the Christian life, and it came back and bit them, hard.

This is a neon sign, flashing a warning right at us: complacency kills.

God Loves A Loser

In the Old Testament we see it from start to finish: again and again, God chooses weak men and women to bring his plans about. Why? So that they never forget their dependence on God.

From Moses to Abraham, David and beyond, the list of weak men and women goes on and on. It's like a heartbeat, and all the time, God is calling me to depend on him, not on my own abilities or resources.

Maybe you've got a job right now that you're not seeing as a long term life investment, just a way to pay the bills, and at the moment you're getting through your shifts by switching onto autopilot.

The Bible instructs us that, whatever we're doing, we should do it for the glory of God (1 Corinthians, 10:31). It doesn't say do *some things* for the glory of God. *Every area* of my life as a Christian is meant to be humbly glorifying him. It's not something I can achieve on autopilot. It requires a continual quest to live each moment in a way that magnifies God.

I'm a father to three girls, and I had a realisation one day when I was praying for them: I can't *make* them love Jesus. It's beyond my control. God was reminding me so that I would feel that sense of dependence on Him. I can't just assume that if I get the Bible out and talk about Jesus every so often then it will happen. God alone is in control, and he wants me to be living with an ongoing understanding of this.

Neil Anderson, author, founder and president of Freedom In Christ Ministries, says: *'The essence of temptation is the invitation to live independently from God'.* Satan knows this; his entire plan has always been to get humans feeling independent - right from the moment Eve looked up at the fruit on the tree, to the moment I got out of bed this morning.

The Freedom Dependence Brings

This is not God hitting us with a stick. Living consciously in the awareness of our dependence on him is the true place for joy like no other. Teacher and author, Bruce Wilkinson, said, *'Dependence on God makes heroes of ordinary people like you and me.'*

If I am secretly slipping into a self-sufficient, casual autopilot attitude at all, it's not just that it's wrong, it also steals joy from my life. Think of how the disciples must have been feeling, surrounded by that crowd who didn't hold back in their criticism and anger at what appeared to be empty claims.

Press PAUSE ⑪

Take a moment to reflect on your week so far: are you feeling that you are able to 'do' the Christian life? Or are you feeling out of your depth and in need of God's power? Be honest - this is just between you and God, and he already knows the truth! Being dependent in this way is meant to free us, to cut through the lie that we're invincible, or even just 'doing ok', that so many of us fall for and feel pressured by.

The Heart of the Issue

If I came across a group of Christians from my church who'd been praying for healing for someone, and that healing hadn't worked - well, I know how I'd probably respond. I'd say something along the lines of *'Nevermind, well done for having a go!'* To me, Jesus response to his disciples is shocking.

"O faithless generation... How long am I to bear with you?... All things are possible for one who believes."

Jesus doesn't say *'Never mind.'* There's no suggestion to try a different technique or use different words. There's no secret recipe for doing the impossible. He sees right to the heart of the issue, and the issue is their hearts.

It's the same today as it was 2,000 years ago: God sees my heart. He doesn't just watch my actions and hear my words superficially, as the world does. He sees my deepest motivations and purposes.

Another thing Jesus doesn't say to his disciples is *'God is sovereign, so he obviously didn't want this demon to be cast out right now'.* How many times have you heard something like that, maybe even said it yourself? We do it all the time, don't we? But Jesus says *'I've given you authority, it's not to do with God's sovereignty: it's that you are faithless!'*

I find it so tempting to try and water those words of Jesus down somehow, to soften the blow - but how can I when Jesus' words are there for all to see?

14

My heart needs to be in a place of deep, abiding, consistent, robust, focussed trust and confidence in a good God who is for me and who will deliver his promises.

Jesus loves these disciples, but he won't mollycoddle them, or us: he won't pretend that Christianity just happens.

Proverbs 4:23 says *'Keep your heart with all vigilance, for from it flow the springs of life.'*

Press PAUSE ⑪

Are you asking God, 'How's my heart?'

Your pastor can't do that for you. Your pastor can be passionate and try and explain the word, but only you can take responsibility before a holy God for the state of your heart.

We're All Losers

Let me make this really clear: there are no 'Super Christians'. Every one of us has the same starting point in Christ, and pastors struggle as much as any other human; the call to Christianity is UNIVERSALLY IMPOSSIBLE for human beings without God.

Charles Spurgeon said, *'I don't think the devil cares how many churches we build, as long as they have lukewarm preachers with lukewarm people.'*

He's right. We could have thousands in every congregation, in thousands of churches, but if we are lukewarm, we will be ineffective. Being lukewarm is another part of being on autopilot; a state where our soul and passion are simply not engaged – indeed, they are withheld from God – and the result is death to our spirits.

Jesus isn't saying *'We all go through lukewarm periods from time to time.'* He's clear on this. I've got to go to war on lukewarm living: I'm not meant to be that way. He doesn't let me off the hook, tell me to chill out and go easy on myself. He is *zealous* for my soul! He yearns to have my full affections and my full trust. He craves it like a father pines for his children who are wayward and giving him all the lip service, but not actually trusting him in their hearts.

I believe God wants to help us. However, in order to smash through our hard hearts and keep them soft, God will not patronize us. Soft platitudes of *'Everything's fine'* produce an autopilot attitude people, with lukewarm hearts.

My heart should be growing in its passion and faithfulness for God. My appetite for him should increasingly be my main appetite in life. If it isn't, then what will happen is what we've just read about in Mark: I'll approach things that are impossible, thinking, *'Maybe I can just blag this'*. But I'll receive a rude awakening again and again. There is no nice, middle ground: we follow Jesus on a radical, narrow path.

And here's where we get bowled over by God's incredible, outrageous, lavish love for us.

Grounded in Grace

Jesus could, at this point, have said 'I'm fed up with you lot! Just go away and I'll find some new guys who'll do better!' But he doesn't say that at all.

These guys are feeling like impotent idiots; they've failed, and they've failed in front of the whole town. And in Mark 9:29, Jesus takes them into a house, to a private place, away from the noise and the circus, and he gives them his full attention, so that they can ask him quietly, *'Why couldn't we cast it out?'* And there, in dignity and privacy, he replies *'This kind cannot be driven out by anything but prayer.'*

And here's our key.

Pray As You Go

There is one answer that Jesus gives here, and we cannot dodge it: it is *prayer*.

However, he's not saying the disciples should have prayed more *in the moment*: by that point it's too late. He's directing them towards an ongoing robust life of prayer.

Joel Virgo used a great illustration in his article for the American-based blog theresurgence.com which described how for these disciples, prayer has become the equivalent of a spare wheel that you get out when your car breaks down. Prayer cannot be your spare wheel: it must be your steering wheel. It has to be the central aspect of your walk with God, when things are good as well as when things are challenging.

This is simply because prayer - asking God and listening for his voice - actually *changes* things. It changes situations around us, but it also changes *internal stuff*. Your prayer life is *directly related* to your spiritual health, your inner faith, your inner passion and your inner confidence in Christ.

I constantly struggle with prayer, so don't feel like you're the only one if you're finding it hard.

One way that autopilot coasting expressed itself in my life was through sleep – just *loving* sleep! Now, sleep is a gift, and something from Jesus – I'm not saying never sleep! It's something we all need, and, believe me, I thank God for it regularly! But there was a time, in those early years of following Jesus, when a love of the comfort of sleep and my bed were standing in the way of my relationship with him, and Jesus spoke to me about it very clearly.

I was at a conference with some other leaders. It was early in the morning and, as usual, my alarm wasn't set. After all, I could easily pray to Jesus all day, any time, wherever I was, right?

Well, yes, of course, that's true. But the problem was, I didn't. And so, my autopilot life carried on. My vulnerability in life marked me out as I had no real deep abiding first love expressed through a consistent prayer life. The love of that simple comfort was dominating my days.

Anyway, back to that conference. As the morning dawned and the dormitory of men snored away, one lone figure silently arose. It was my friend, Joel. Where was he going so early?, I wondered. Had his bladder forced him out of bed? If so, why was he gathering up his stuff? And then it dawned on me: I was watching a disciplined prayer life happen, and it was as simple and simultaneously as difficult as just getting out of bed a bit earlier and doing it.

Again and again, throughout church history, prayer is the single activity that is lifted up as the consistent reason for God doing great things.

John Wesley said *'God does nothing except in response to believing prayer.'*

S. D. Gordon says *'The greatest thing anyone can do for God or man is to pray'*

Chuck Smith says *'The most important thing a born again Christian can do is pray'*

For many Christians, prayer feels like an uphill struggle. You're certainly not alone if that's you. Let's look together at some of the reasons for this battle, which I feel are pretty crucial to us in our current generation.

The Business of Busyness

Busyness: doesn't sound very spiritual, does it? But I think it's probably the number one reason that most of us don't pray.

The intense pace of 21st century living is one of the biggest enemies to your soul being nourished with prayer, and therefore it is an obstacle to you being faithful, and consequently able to do the things of God. You can trace the pattern here.

If we look back over the last few hundred years, we begin to understand the extraordinary days we are living in right now.

Sociologists tell us that the average human now in the western world is exposed to 5,000 media messages every single day. That's text messages, phones, the internet, television, the news, magazines... It is overwhelming. The technical name for all of this is 'clutter'. The biggest enemy to your development in God is simply 'clutter'. It is information overload, and we're so acclimatized to this clutter that we don't even know it's unusual.

We live in this extraordinary sliver of time in history, compared with the ages that have gone, where we are being bombarded, bombarded, bombarded, and the enemy loves it, while we're barely even conscious of it.

Apparently, if someone reads a paper every day for seven days, they will have consumed more information than the average person would have done in their entire life a hundred years ago! That's how much information we are being blasted with today. The average American watches between five to eight hours of TV every day, while in the UK the Broadcasters Audience Research Board reports that it's around four and a half.

All this has an effect in terms of God's relationship with us and our ability to hear from him.

I once heard a story about a guy who was getting married and he was standing at the altar, when someone noticed he had a hands-free phone set on his ear! He's at the altar waiting for his bride to come!

And when questioned about it he said he had a pretty important call that could have come, so he wanted to make use of the time, just in case.

You and I live in an age that is addicted to information.

Look at the friends meeting in coffee shops, eyes flicking between their lattes and their mobiles while conducting their closest relationships.

It sounds silly, but as simple as it is, turning my phone off for serious chunks of time and turning off my computer does something to my soul. It gives me the space to slow down and allow God to be heard once again.

In Matthew 6:6, Jesus says, *'When you pray, go into your room and shut the door.'* We can ponder the deep meaning of this, or we can face the simple necessity of spending significant chunks of time alone with God, without any distractions or impediments.

Give It Time

For most of us, when we start praying we feel about as spiritual as a bag of wet cement.

I start in the 'flesh', that is, trapped in the physical reality of being human. My mind wants to tick a million things off that day's to-do list, but I must pull it back, forcing it to focus on God rather than myself. Suddenly, something happens and I'm connecting with my Heavenly Father, and I sense something shifting. But there's always that initial effort to be made, it takes an act of will to get me praying in the first place.

Corrie Ten Boom says this: *'Don't pray when you feel like it, have an appointment with the Lord and keep to it.'* She's really practical about it. There's nothing wrong with praying when you're in the mood, but have a life where you are actually putting in place regular daily time with God, and be prepared to persist, expecting to feel like that bag of cement when you start, but also expecting to meet with God and sense that change in your spirit, as *'deep calls to deep'* (Psalm 42:7).

Ignorance is Anything but Bliss

Our second reason for the lack of a robust, exciting prayer life is ignorance.

Firstly, ignorance about the *power* of prayer.

Prayer is not only being with God, it is about asking God for things, again and again and again. In John 15:16, Jesus said *'You did not choose me, but I chose you and appointed you that you should bear fruit, and that your fruit should abide, so that whatever you ask the father in my name, he may give it to you.'*

Terry Virgo, founder of New Frontiers International, says that verse tells him that *'This is my identity as a Christian: I am a hand-picked 'asker.' I've been picked by God and my job is to ask him.'*

That is our identity. We are those that ask God, because there is enormous, incredible power available when we ask God to do the things that he's promised to do. He doesn't do things that he hasn't promised to do, but when we say to him, *'God, you told us through this'*, or *'You said it through a prophetic word and Lord, I believe you,'* something powerful happens in our relationship with him. It's not about twisting God's arm: it's about working with God in His purposes.

The great apostle Paul had pretty impressive spiritual credentials: the way he became a Christian was by the risen Lord himself appearing to him and knocking him off a horse, then blinding him and restoring his sight. He was certainly familiar with miraculous happenings, and yet his constant, repeated request to the churches he writes to is *'Pray for me, pray for me, pray for me'*. Why? Because he knows there is power in prayer!

Paul agrees with you and me that prayer is a battle – that's why he uses language like *'strive together with me,'* (Romans 15:30). It's not easy, but we must give ourselves to it. It's not enough to want to do it or to know that we should do it, we have to actually do it.

The Powers That Be

One thing that you can be sure of when you take action and actually start to pray is that the enemy will wage war: your flesh, the world, everything will try and work against you and me seeing this as something that we move forward in. And why will the enemy wage war? Because of the very power that exists in prayer!

'Satan trembles when he sees the weakest Christian on his knees,' said the Anglican clergyman, William Cooper.

The Wesleyan Methodist minister, Samuel Chadwick, said this: *The only concern of the devil is to keep Christians from praying. He fears nothing from prayer-less studies. Nothing from prayer-less work. Nothing from prayer-less religion. He laughs at our toil, he mocks our wisdom, but he trembles when we pray.'*

Charles Spurgeon was probably one of the greatest preachers that ever lived, but he knew the difference a praying Christian makes. That's why he said, *'I would rather teach one man to pray than ten men to preach.'*

If you made the decision as of this day to not just listen to another sermon on prayer, or read another book about prayer, but to actually change your week and devote yourself to prayer - then the Bible, and its greatest proclaimers, promise this is the wisest choice that you can make in your life.

You can make that decision today, at this exact moment. Simply say, *'Lord, even now, help me to see how my life can be structured differently so that I can honour the principle of prayer. I'm going do something in my small group, in my family, with my friends, we're going to become a people who pray.'*

Otherwise, as we hurtle through the year, we will be like the disciples at this moment of Mark's gospel account: our churches might have cool websites and all the right-sounding talk and the high-fiving feel-good factor imaginable - and no power! I don't want people to come to my church expecting life transformation, only to discover there's no power there.

God wants every single Christian to have a deep abiding prayer life, which means their faith levels are high, and they're in a place of certainty that, *'If we pray for your situation then, my friend, we will see change.'* He doesn't just want it to be a few super-keenies, he wants to see the whole church equipped in faith, he wants to hear us saying and meaning, Yes! We can move mountains! We can see those people who thought Christ was the most irrelevant person in their lives come to know the living God!

God's passion is *for* you: he doesn't want you to be lukewarm: he can't work with you in autopilot, self-dependency mode. He wants you right now to take away this very uncomplicated thing: *learn to pray!*

Give yourself to prayer.

Know Who You're Praying To

Another sort of ignorance is a forgetting of who it is that we're praying *to*.

At the end of Mark 9, in verse 31, Jesus says this: *The Son of Man is going to be delivered into the hands of men. They will kill him, and after three days he will rise.*' It's a very particular choice of word: *delivered.*

When your postman or woman delivers a parcel to you, they place it in your hands. So, who's going to deliver Jesus?

On one level it will be Judas, who betrays him. On another level, the Jewish leaders will deliver him to be killed. But the implication of this is incredibly profound: who will ultimately deliver Jesus Christ to be killed for your sin and mine? It's his Father.

If you're a parent, maybe you've got a particular privilege with being able to emotionally connect with the idea of delivering up your child to be killed. I can't even conceive of it. I cannot conceive of the love of the Father for *me*, that he would deliver up *his Son* to die for *me*. And why? So that I could *pray* to him! So that you and I could have a direct communication with God!

It wasn't a cheap thing for you to be able to pray to God: it cost him the life of his Son. For us not to pray is not only unwise and leads to a lack of power, but it breaks the heart of the God who adores us.

When I pray, I am talking to my Father, who doesn't love me in a general, vague way: He loved me enough to give up his precious Son. God only had one son, and he gave him up to die for me and for you, so that we could be wherever we are today, and talk to him, and he wouldn't pour out his wrath, but he'd silence heaven to listen to us. Our tender loving Father strains his ear to hear. He delights in our asking, because as we ask we get closer to him, and he gets the chance to respond. He rejoices when we silence the busyness of life. He loves it when we're not just cocky and arrogant and presumptuous; he yearns for us to ask of him.

The biggest secret with prayer is *knowing who you are praying to:* that's the gospel.

Risen to the Challenge

As ever with the gospel, it's a challenge to our comfortable lifestyles. Some of what we've looked at in this chapter has been about *doing stuff*, and the danger when you talk about *doing stuff* is that you see a long list, like New Year's Resolutions that you've no hope of keeping.

Christianity is not a to-do list. Everything we do is all in the context of grace, of God first loving you, dying for you, beating death for you, opening a way for you. Remember, we are *not* the heroes in this scenario.

But that grace should never be an excuse to live a sloppy life this side of eternity, where I set aside intentional time for TV and social media, but rarely tend to my soul through prayer.

We are not living in peace time; if you love Christ, there is a good fight that he is calling you to. A fight for peace, against evil, to see God's Kingdom come and his love set people free. A fight in which prayer is our secret, massive, incredible weapon. Nobody can ever take away your right to pray and commune with the God who adores you, because Jesus, through his death, made a way for you and for me, for all time.

We need to see our prayer lives grow and mature not just because it sounds good, but because this passage is telling us that unless we are faithful in this discipline, we will lack the power that we need to change our world forever.

God wants to be with us; He wants to help us; but we have to ask.

Check Your Reality

Use this space to journal your thoughts:

How would you describe your prayer life at this point in your walk with Christ?

_____

_____

_____

_____

What gets in the way of, or prevents you, from praying?

_____

_____

_____

_____

Which verse (or verses) from this chapter have particularly spoken to you or caught your attention?

_____

_____

_____

_____

God speaks through his word: what is he saying to you today through this verse?

_____

_____

_____

_____

If you viewed your life as a prayer, with each action and thought an act of worship and a cry to see God's kingdom come, how could your day look today?

_____

_____

_____

_____

_____

Try it yourself...

❖ When you're struggling to 'get into' prayer, start by declaring out loud some truths about God, eg 'You sent your Son to die for me', 'You loved me before the universe began' to set your focus on who you are praying to.

❖ Pray the Lord's Prayer regularly. It's the model given to us directly by Jesus - so you can trust its authenticity and power. He wouldn't have taught it to us if it wasn't important or true.

❖ If it helps, you might like to read a Psalm or listen to some worship music to still the busyness of your day and get you into a quieter frame of mind. Find a song that helps you shift from busyness to rest, and to focus your thoughts on Jesus.

❖ Try taking five minutes every day to sit in silence and rest before God. Prayer isn't one way traffic, it's a conversation. Don't you hate it when someone rants at you and then goes away without listening to anything you might have to say? Sit quietly, let God know you are listening for his voice, and wait in silence for five minutes. Many times you will find your mind wandering, so choose a word that you can use as an anchor, to refocus yourself. Make this word an aspect of God that you want to know more of – perhaps 'peace' or 'joy'. This exercise changes your prayer life, because it gives God a chance to speak to you while he has your full attention!

❖ Prayer is an ongoing conversation. Chat to God in the silence of your heart all day, praise and worship him as you travel, work, eat, exercise… whatever you're doing, allow God into your life and the lives of others through this secret, massive, incredible weapon!

❖ Keep it simple: overcomplicating prayer can put us off even starting.

❖ Ironically, if you struggle with prayer, the best thing to do is to pray about that! Ask God to help you to pray. If you're feeling lukewarm, ask him to rescue you from that. If you're feeling numb inside, detached from him, ask him to help you care about the state of your heart and to increase your intimacy with him. If you're struggling to believe, echo the words of the father who receives the answer to his prayer in this passage: "Help me in my unbelief!"

Take it further

Recommended reading:

On Prayer by E.M. Bounds

Just Like Us by Stef Liston

Prayer by Philip Yancy

How To Pray: A Simple Guide for Normal People by Pete Greig

Red Moon Rising by Pete Greig

… There's loads more great books though: ask Christian friends, or your pastor, for their recommendations.

Chapter Two

Mark 10: 17–31

Being a Seeker Isn't Enough

'And as he was setting out on his journey, a man ran up and knelt before him and asked him, "Good teacher, what must I do to inherit eternal life?" And Jesus said to him, "Why do you call me good? No one is good except God alone. You know the commandments: 'Do not murder, Do not commit adultery, Do not steal, Do not bear false witness, Do not de-fraud, Honour your father and mother.'" And he said to him, "Teacher, all these I have kept from my youth." And Jesus, looking at him, loved him, and said to him, "You lack one thing: go, sell all that you have and give to the poor, and you will have treasure in heaven; and come, follow me." Disheartened by the saying, he went away sorrowful, for he had great possessions.

And Jesus looked around and said to his disciples, "How difficult it will be for those who have wealth to enter the kingdom of God!" And the disciples were amazed at his words. But Jesus said to them again, "Children, how difficult it is to enter the kingdom of God! It is easier for a camel to go through the eye of a needle than for a rich person to enter the kingdom of God." And they were exceedingly astonished, and said to him, "Then who can be saved?" Jesus looked at them and said, "With man it is impossible, but not with God. For all things are possible with God." Peter began to say to him, "See, we have left everything and followed you." Jesus said, "Truly, I say to you, there is no one who has left house or brothers or sisters or mother or father or children or lands, for my sake and for the gospel, who will not receive a hundredfold now in this time, houses and brothers and sisters and mothers and children and lands, with persecutions, and in the age to come eternal life. But many who are first will be last, and the last first."

I have a feeling this young man would probably fit in very well in most churches across the Western world: how about you? He seems like a genuinely nice guy; moral, humble and earnestly thinking about the big issues of life. He's someone I'd like to have in my church and small group, someone I'd enjoy chatting with over a coffee.

But this passage reveals a very sobering truth. As good as it is to have an *internal* heart that is seeking after God, when Jesus asks this young man to make an *external* step to demonstrate his desire for God - when he's asked to *actually do* something - he fails. He cannot bring himself to obey Christ at the moment when it really counts.

Once again, Jesus reveals what a deadly enemy we have in comfort. Following him isn't just about internal contemplation on God and his commands. There are times when Jesus calls us to take specific, external steps to demonstrate the reality of our love for him. Being a seeker, as good as it is, simply isn't enough.

Character Study

There are several clues in this passage that tell us something about this young man's character.

Verse 17 tells us he *'ran up'* to Jesus. That may not sound too whacky, but in that culture if you were a man with some prestige and status, you didn't *run* anywhere. Running was something kids did: Real Men *walked*. So this young man is clearly eager and enthusiastic. He's so keen to find out about God, he'll risk looking a bit daft in order to do so. So far, so good.

Next we see that he *'knelt before him'*. Again, this is an extraordinary act of *humility*. He's keen, but he's also humble. If we want to find out about the things of God, one of the greatest themes in scripture is humility. This young man has clearly grasped that. He's still impressing me.

But it gets even better! When his moment to ask Jesus his question comes, he says this: *'Good teacher, what must I do to inherit eternal life?'* So he's not only got lots going on in this life, but he's also starting to think about the life to come. That's rare! So many people go through life without really thinking about what happens after they die. But this young man is thinking seriously, with real earnestness and humility about God's eternal plans.

And so verse 21 should come as no surprise: *'And Jesus, looking at him, loved him.'*

Jesus *loves* him!

I just want to take this opportunity to say - and forgive me if this sounds a bit obvious - but Jesus *really loves you*. He looks at you, and he *loves* you. Never let go of the reality of his love for you.

So what is the most *loving* thing that Jesus can reply to this man who's seeking a 'spiritual life'? He looks at him and he says 'Sell all that you have and give your money to the poor.'

How does this response leave you feeling? Do you think Jesus is being harsh?

Or do you suspect that Jesus is after his money? Is that what was really going on here?

The bible tells us that Jesus is God, and that he created and sustains all things. He was the cause of the dawn this morning, he made the birds in the air, the rivers, the mountains - he made the beautiful things that we see, know and touch. He sustains Pluto, Jupiter, Mars and Earth; in short, he doesn't need this man's money.

He wants something else.

When you follow God there are always - both at the beginning and until the day you die - these kinds of moments. These times when you need to go deep, and you need to respond to God with more than your lips.

What's Your Issue?

Maybe money is a big issue for you. But it might just as easily be something else.

It could be your reputation.

That was the big thing for me, when I was looking into becoming a Christian. I was an atheist and proud. All my friends were atheists, and we looked down on Christians as being a bit weird. I remember feeling physical terror at the thought of having to tell others about my change of heart. For months after I became a Christian, I worshipped in a state of conflict, hearing a little voice in my head saying, *What are you doing?* I had to put that issue on the altar and say, *Lord, I know that for me to follow you requires that I give my anxieties about my reputation to you.'*

Maybe it's sex.

I remember meeting with a young lady who was just like this rich young ruler in many ways. She'd been a Christian for a while, and she was really seeking. She knew her bible better than most people, and she was earnest. But she was living with her boyfriend, and their relationship was sexual.

Over many months she and I and the girl who mentored her would meet up. Her mentor and I would very gently ask, what do you think the bible says about this issue? We tried so hard to help her to understand that she had to talk to her boyfriend about this situation, that it wasn't just ok for it to endlessly go on. In the end she said *'If I stop having sex with him, he'll walk away, and I need him'*, and she went away sorrowful.

Press PAUSE ⑩

What's the challenge in your life?

Don't make the mistake of thinking this is just for when you first become a Christian. This is part of the ongoing journey of love that God takes us on when we allow him into our lives.

When Jesus looked at this rich young ruler he knew that for this specific man, the king on the throne of his heart was materialism: acquiring and owning *stuff*.

Turning Points

Two key elements of the Christian walk are *faith* and *repentance*. Faith is this trust and belief in God that he alone can save us. But this faith must express itself through something called repentance, where we act upon that belief and we, both internally and externally, change our direction in life. We do different things, we value different things - our lifestyle changes: that's repentance. And that's what this rich young ruler fails to do. He has some sort of faith in God - some sort of belief - but when it comes to changing his lifestyle, tragically he walks away from God.

Jesus is picking out the issue of money for this man, because he knows it's the single most important issue here. It's not that if the rich young ruler gave the money away he would somehow then *earn* his way to being a 'proper' Christian.

Jesus is asking which is the greater love for him: God or possessions. And to cut straight to the heart of the matter, he asks him to give them all up. That's the barrier between him and God and it's holding him back in terms of his faith journey as surely as if he nailed one foot to the floor and then tried to go out for a walk.

Heart And Soul

The true issue is that his heart is so bound to his material comforts for security, identity and meaning that he finds himself unable to even consider walking away from it. And as we see the hold that wealth has on this man's heart, it all gets a bit scary.

Jesus isn't just some sort of nice guy. He's loving, but he's also wildly confrontational, and his diagnosis is precise: *'You've got to sell everything, so serious is this situation - selling some stuff and keeping some won't help you at all!'* And then in verse 23 he says this: *'How difficult it will be for those who have wealth to enter the kingdom of God!'*

Now his disciples are really confused, because Jewish thinking was that if you had money then you were blessed. Money and material wealth were seen to mean that you were loved more by God. They're looking at Jesus at this moment in utter confusion.

So Jesus repeats himself, and he finally says, in verse 27: *'With man it is impossible.'*

There is something about wealth that he's nailing here which is frightening.

I have a funny feeling that you're reading this right now and thinking, *'Good job I'm not rich. Phew!'* And I'm fairly confident of this assumption, because *I feel the same way myself!*

Rich Pickings

We all think we're not rich, because we compare ourselves to the J.K.Rowlings, Richard Bransons or Bill Gates of this world. You might even be picturing someone fairly well off in your church right now, and you're thinking, *man, they really need to read this!*

Unfortunately, that's all part of the comfort delusion.

Over 50% of the world live on £1 a day. If you've got any kind of job, you probably earn a lot more than that. The average person in the world would look at most of us in the Western church who say, *'I'm broke,'* and would think we're either sick or mad.

Billy Graham, the great evangelist, said *'You're rich if you've had a meal today.'* He wasn't just being provocative. We have absolutely no idea as to how privileged we are compared with the vast majority of people in the world. We are unbelievably wealthy, and what Jesus tells us here repeatedly is this: if you're wealthy, you are at a profound *spiritual disadvantage.*

Riches blind us about our past, our present and our future.

The Lies Wealth Tells

Riches blind me to the reality of God's grace in my past when my soul concludes that I have achieved my wealth through hard work and by earning it myself.

Wealth murmurs to me, *'You've worked hard! You deserve this success!'.* It whispers lies which effectively amount to, *'You are independent,'* a self-sufficiency which consigns God to the Sunday sidelines. It's a profound, terrifying lie.

Looking back at our rich young ruler in Mark 10, it's interesting that Jesus says, *'You lack one thing.'* That one thing is neither generosity nor austerity: it's a sense of dependence upon God. This young man didn't live with a sense of being desperately in need of God to sustain him for each day. That's what wealth does. It numbs our sense of need for God, and dulls our dependence upon him. It blinds us to the reality of our situation.

A Matter of Perspective

It's notable also, that when this rich young man calls Jesus, he calls him a *'Teacher.'* He doesn't say *'Saviour.'* He doesn't say *'I know I need rescuing, and you're the one who can save me.'* He says, *'You're a teacher'*, it's more like peer group language: *'I need someone to give me a bit of advice, I need someone to 'tweak' me. I've got most of my life sorted but there's this kind of moral, God-aspect and I need a little bit of help on that, if that's ok, Jesus.'*

Bronnie Ware, who worked in palliative care for many years, wrote a book called *The Top Five Regrets of the Dying - A Life Transformed by the Dearly Departing* (published by Hay House UK). The regrets were as follows:

1: I wish I'd had the courage to live a life true to myself, not the life others expected of me.

2: I wish I hadn't worked so hard.

3: I wish I'd had the courage to express my feelings.

4: I wish I'd stayed in touch with my friends.

5: I wish I'd let myself be happier.

Those are five tweaks right there! The biggest regrets of most people dying are tweaks! *My life's basically ok, I'm not that bad, I just need a little bit of a tweak'.* Getting right with God and preparing for eternity doesn't even make the list!

This is what wealth and possessions can whisper to us. They delude us about the power we have over our own lives, because we can cushion ourselves against pain and need, and they blur our vision for anything bigger than ourselves because our immediate physical needs are all met.

Present Tense

Wealth not only blurs our vision, it also blinds us regarding our present. Jesus *loved* the rich young man, and he *loves* us. He loves us too much to let us live with the delusions of comfort.

Wealth allows us to live like zombies, spending our days in a lukewarm, oblivious state. God is heartbroken over lukewarm Christians! He doesn't shrug his shoulders and say, *'Never mind, it happens to us all eventually'* - he's *heartbroken*! You might have the best designer clothes and the latest technology and a great house and car and everything that you could physically desire, but if your soul is lukewarm before God, you're being ripped off! Your comfortable physical state means that you are potentially being deceived about the quality of your spiritual life *right now.*

Imagine you went to a friend's house and found him sitting on his sofa, watching TV. On the screen he's staring at, there is an indecipherable, fuzzy picture, with sound all over the place. You say, *'Woah, what are you doing?'* and he replies, *'I'm watching TV, of course! This is what the cable man told me TV should be like!'* You'd say, *'My friend, you are being ripped off; your experience of watching TV should not be like that, it should be like this -'* and you'd put him right, wouldn't you? Because he's being robbed of the full-colour experience he should be having.

When Jesus looks down on his church, and sees how lukewarm we are, he says, *'You are unwittingly profoundly deceived about the quality of your spiritual life.'* Material comforts allow us to carry on, doped-up, zoned out and lukewarm.

Back to the Future

Material wealth tricks us as to the amount of control we've had over our lives so far, it robs us of the full experience of dependence on God in the present and, finally, it blinds us regarding eternity. We're supposed to be storing our treasures in heaven (Matthew 6:19-20), not focusing on our bank accounts here on earth. And, as we see here, an inability to loosen his grip on his possessions meant that this young man walked away from Christ filled with sorrow.

He has been offered 'treasure in heaven' by Jesus, who is standing right there in the flesh, but the stuff he has on earth has too tight a hold on him, and prevents him from receiving it.

The danger is that we can feel challenged over this, and then go and make a cup of tea, send a text, and forget all about it. Our lives could continue without a single change taking place. We'll say, *'Phew! I felt really challenged over that! So, what shall we have for tea tonight?'*

Let's call time on complacency.

Only *you* can take responsibility for your own heart before God, only you can do whatever it takes because you don't want to face God one day in a lukewarm state. God has offered you eternal relationship with him, the price for which was the death of his only son. There should be no contest between a relationship with the God of the universe and *stuff*.

Obviously, I don't know where you're at with this. You might be really clear on it and flying high, and God bless you if you are. But do you know what, *I* need to hear this; I don't *feel* like I'm rich! My goodness I don't - but statistically I *am*. And therefore I have to say to God, '*Lord, check my heart!*'

It's full on, isn't it? It's hardcore, radical and confrontational. Again, Jesus is calling us to live a life that, in our own power, is simply not possible; it's too hard for us.

The good news is, this isn't the end of the story. Jesus in his mercy and grace, and his stunning kindness, doesn't just say, '*No more chances, you've blown it!*'

Mission Impossible

In Mark 10:27, Jesus says: 'With man it is impossible, but not with God. For all things are possible with God.'

So here's the hope. There's the challenge we've got to feel: allow it to affect your soul. But there is also the beautiful wisdom of God providing a way by which rich people - that's you and me - can know and grow in him.

It's a miracle! Statistically it's incredibly unlikely, is what the bible says, but it can happen, and it involves us repenting: turning our hearts and then our lives away from the direction we were going and instead choosing to follow Jesus' direction. There are three very simple ways of giving shown in scripture, and they involve our wallets.

Giving to Feel.

Firstly, I need to give so that I feel my dependency. This nails that first type of blindness, the past tense one, and was, as we saw, the one thing that this man lacked; a sense of his dependence upon God.

People who don't feel needy don't see Jesus as a saviour; they see him as a teacher. They see Christianity as something that's helpful and additional, full of wise words and thoughts; not as an incredible expression of mercy towards someone in desperate need of a loving redeemer.

You and I are *needy people* - that's the bottom line! God wanted this rich young ruler - and he wants me - to develop a lifestyle of giving in such a way that isn't just logically feasible. He wants me to give so that it makes me feel really scared and dependent! God wants me to understand that I am dependent upon him for the next breath I take.

I inhale - and I exhale: okay, his mercy is still here. And again? Okay, he's still sustaining me. It's as simple as that.

I have a friend, Phil Moore, who leads a church in South London, and he says: '...*I love to give in such a way that after I've given I come back to my seat and I don't want to worship: I want to vomit.*'

So often I can think, '*Well, I've got this worked out and it will mean we've got those savings for this and that account to fall back on and blah, blah, blah*' - but it's so insipid! God doesn't want me to be feeling self-sufficient, he wants me to become aware of my increasing dependence on him. The older I get, the more I should realise it.

And as I give in a way where I *feel* my dependence, I grow closer and closer to the God who loves me in a way that makes material wealth look pathetic.

Some years ago, I was at a youth event attended by around 6,000 teenagers. One of the climaxes of the week was the offering. When it was announced it would happen, my honest feeling was, 'Oh no!' I genuinely felt pretty hard up at the time, and the thought of giving any kind of money away was not appealing. I was a poor student, and surely could be excused from this kind of activity? Jesus would understand!

And then it happened: the guy leading this bit of the event sat down on the stage, and in the most understated way possible just chatted with us. He talked through why we give. He spoke about the joy of giving, of actually trusting Jesus with our lives. Of letting go of the delusions of control by letting go of cash. He told us that giving was actually *fun*. He said that following Jesus into this daring moment, whilst scary, was ultimately a gift. A way of loosening the delusion we can all succumb to that our money provides us with security, and that our savings are a legitimate place to put our hopes.

In those five minutes, God mercifully ambushed me. My heart was undone. The amount I thought I'd give quickly doubled, then trebled, then quadrupled. I was drunk in the Spirit of God! I was drunk in love, absolutely intoxicated with a sense of Jesus' joy and intimacy over my life that meant signing that cheque was not even the slightest challenge.

All glory to him, all honour to him who would do a miracle in the heart of a Scrooge like me! It was like I was watching myself! And you know, although I can't say every time I give is exactly like that, in many ways it is just like that. It's a moment when God works deeply in me in a tangible way that releases and breaks an orphan-hearted delusion and releases a fresh trust that I am *HIS!* I am his beloved son, and as a child of God, just like Jesus, I am now secure, affirmed and provided for.

The Present is a Gift

I also give so that I can receive true riches in the present. In verse 29, Jesus says: *'Truly, I say to you there is no one who has left house or brother or sisters or mother or father or children or land for my sake and for the gospel, who will not receive a hundredfold now, in this time, houses brothers, sisters, mothers and children and land, with persecutions, and in the age to come eternal life.'*

That is a promise to me and you from the lips of Jesus Christ. If I give - and he broadens it, not just to giving money - if I've left relationships and family ties and things that potentially were going to be a greater love to me than loving Christ, then I should be expectant that in this lifetime, he will reward me a hundredfold!

Now, I'm not a prosperity teacher. God sometimes does, in his grace, give wealth back, (in order that I may give more) but that's not really the heart of Jesus here. He gives us spiritual wealth, spiritual riches. I don't think there is a truer, more beautiful treasure in this life than a deep, abiding, passionate, ever growing, ever maturing relationship with God. I want that above everything else - who wouldn't? I want it above the hollow things of this world that give momentary pleasure and are then just boring, instantly not what we hoped they would be. God wants me to learn this now, quickly, rather than spend my life half in one camp and half in the other. He wants me to know that true spiritual return on my investment is a deep abiding relationship with God in his family.

God's love for us is breathtaking.

Take Zacchaeus, in Luke 19. He's a tax collector, and he's loaded, because he's been swindling people for years. When Jesus calls him down from that tree and goes to his house and speaks to him about a relationship with God, a light goes on inside him. He's a million miles away from this rich young ruler with his deliberations and weighing up and sorrow: Zacchaeus is over the moon, and spontaneously gives half of everything away. He then says anyone I've ripped off I'm going to give half of it back, no double it, no, quadruple it! It's like a fountain springing up: he used to have material wealth, and now he realises he has spiritual wealth.

Wealth now looks like a rusty, boring, dead thing to him. There's only one power that can loosen our souls from the love of stuff, and it's the spiritual wealth of knowing Jesus: it's about knowing the joy.

If you're lukewarm you might be saying to yourself, I need to pray more. Or maybe you're saying to yourself I need to read my bible more. Both those things are good, but what we're seeing here is that maybe you need to give more! Giving is a gift from God and it's gloriously practical: as you give, God has promised to bless you. And if the blessing is wealth, then the great joy is that you have more to give!

Jesus wasn't a rich man. One time when he was teaching, he asked *'Has anyone got a denarius?'* A denarius is a coin, a day's wage: he didn't have one! And yet at the same time the disciples had a money bag that they carried with them for the poor. Think about that: God on earth didn't have a denarius, but he had a money bag that he used to give to the poor.

When he was born, it was in an animal's feeding trough in a stable; when he was buried, it was in a borrowed tomb. He repeatedly said, *'The Son of Man has nowhere to lay his head.'* He didn't own a home. There's something that God's trying to tell us here - there's an equation in heaven that doesn't always add up in earthly logic.

Jesus was the wealthiest man in history in terms of spiritual wealth. He understood that equation, that there's no contest between a loving, trusting relationship with his father and anything else at all that could try and tempt his soul away from that.

From Here To Eternity

Thirdly, and finally, we give so that we receive true riches in eternity.

Look at Jesus' words to the rich young ruler, '...*you will have treasure in heaven.*'

We'll be in heaven a lot longer than we're here on earth, and these are treasures beyond any earthly imaginings: treasure that God calls *treasure* will far outweigh anything humans call treasure.

I can try and work out what that might be with my tiny brain, but I think I'd be working it out forever. It's meant to catch my heart! It's meant to fill my soul with the sense that, whatever this is, it's good!

This is an invitation to ask God by his Holy Spirit to enable us to conquer the things that hold us back. Don't listen to the voice that says, '*You're just going to stay the same forever*', or, '*You don't have much money, this doesn't apply to you.*' This is about the battle for your soul! It's an ongoing process that God always brings us back to. God loves you more than any possession ever could. He is gentle and kind and full of grace, and he wants us to live in true freedom. He knows that money and possessions trap and enslave us, and he doesn't want us to be slaves. It's not about guilt, it's all about love and liberation.

Mastering this opens up our lives to God's grace in our past, his sustaining power today, and our hope of a future with him.

The Conversion of the Wallet

Martin Luther, the German monk who became a seminal figure in the protestant reformation, spoke about how we all have three conversions in our life, conversion of the head, conversion of the heart, conversion of the wallet. For some of us, that third conversion has not happened yet, or it has in the past, but we've got to go back to it. This isn't just something that's a private issue, it's one of the consistent traits in the great men and women who have changed the world; it seems to be something that they all understood and acted upon.

People like Charles T. Studd, whose father was one of the wealthiest people in England. Charles grew up, went to Eton and Cambridge, and then played cricket for England. In 1882, everything was going right for him, he was effectively sports personality of the year, and he was flying high.

In 1883, he read Mark chapter 10, and he was totally undone. He had inherited £170,000 (remember this is 200 years ago, so it would be millions in today's value) and he immediately gave 90 per cent of it away. He gave 45 per cent to some of the poorest people in India, and he gave 45 per cent to the poor in London. He just kept back ten per cent, £17,000.

He was about to get married to his fiancé, Prescilla, and so he told her what he'd done. She responded by saying, '*Oh, Charlie, Jesus didn't say to the rich young ruler 'give 90 per cent away': he said give it all away. Come on, let's start our marriage with a clear conscience before our God.*' And so they joyfully gave away the last £17,000 of the fortune, and they started their married life with £5. They then left England, and went to China, and poured their lives into obscurity, barely with clothes on their backs, and yet they preached riches in Christ.

I find that seriously challenging. My deepest heart's desire is that we would all be Charlie and Prescilla Studds. God wants us to shake our lives up. Seeking, listening, hearing, knowing isn't enough. There needs to be obedience, there need to be steps, there need to be decisions made. And for this young guy, it cost him his salvation. That is terrifying. His love for stuff ultimately led him to walk away from Christ.

Money Culture

Imagine if your church had a culture where people looked in and said, 'This church doesn't make any sense! There's a culture shift that's different here. They're not slaves to their cash-flow like the world is. There's something going on here!'

That will change the world. We can talk, talk, talk and explain things - and that's good! But when people see a church giving, they will have to ask 'Why?' It's the biggest 'god' of this world, money. If I say, 'It does not control me - I trust in my redeemer. I trust that when I step out in faith, even when it seems crazy, he will not let my foot slip,' that will speak volumes about who God really is.

We've looked at wealth here, but there's lots of things that we put our trust in and so allow to control our lives. It's not just money, it's the stuff it gets for us, and the sense of control and security we find in those things.

We must keep checking our hearts on this, and never stop asking God to unveil our eyes to see the delusions of material comfort.

Check Your Reality

Use this space to journal your thoughts:

Do you 'feel' rich? Why, or why not?

_____

_____

_____

_____

_____

What is the 'stuff' that has a hold on you? For example, technology, home comforts, music, books, cars etc.

_____

_____

_____

_____

_____

Are there other non-physical things that you hold onto too tightly at the cost of following Christ? For example, social media, exercising, reputation, work, status, children, partner, friends… can you think of any others?

_____

_____

_____

_____

_____

Write a wish-list of things you'd like to own in the left-hand column below. In the right-hand column, write a list of the treasures God offers you. How do the two compare?

Try It Yourself...

❖ Give to live! Put it into practice; give so that you feel your dependence upon God. Unfortunately, there's no watering it down: Jesus is radical, don't be lukewarm. Keep your heart in check, and your wallet open. Live generously in the small things, and see what God can do with whatever you give to him. Look for opportunities to be generous.

❖ Pray, pray, pray! Don't forget – we can't do this on autopilot! Pray and ask for God's help in this area, as you seek to be obedient, ask for a fresh revelation of his heart for the poor, and his heart for your wallet, and his heart for your life.

Take it Further

Recommended reading:

Money, Possessions and Eternity by Randy Alcorn

Rich Christians in an Age of Hunger by Ronald Sider

C.T. Studd, Cricketer and Pioneer by Norman P. Grubb

Chapter Three

Mark 10: 32–45

It's Not About You

'And they were on the road, going up to Jerusalem, and Jesus was walking ahead of them. And they were amazed, and those who followed were afraid. And taking the twelve again, he began to tell them what was to happen to him, saying, "See, we are going up to Jerusalem, and the Son of Man will be delivered over to the chief priests and the scribes, and they will condemn him to death and deliver him over to the Gentiles. And they will mock him and spit on him, and flog him and kill him. And after three days he will rise."

And James and John, the sons of Zebedee, came up to him and said to him, "Teacher, we want you to do for us whatever we ask of you." And he said to them, "What do you want me to do for you?" And they said to him, "Grant us to sit, one at your right hand and one at your left, in your glory." Jesus said to them, "You do not know what you are asking. Are you able to drink the cup

that I drink, or to be baptized with the baptism with which I am baptized?"
And they said to him, "We are able." And Jesus said to them, "The cup that I
drink you will drink, and with the baptism with which I am baptized, you will be
baptized, but to sit at my right hand or at my left is not mine to grant, but it is
for those for whom it has been prepared." And when the ten heard it, they began
to be indignant at James and John. And Jesus called them to him and said, "You
know that those who are considered rulers of the Gentiles lord it over them, and
their great ones exercise authority over them. But it shall not be so among you.
But whoever would be great among you must be your servant, and whoever would
be first among you must be slave of all. For even the Son of Man came not to be
served, but to serve, and to give his life as a ransom for many."

Freaking Out Yet?

If you've been feeling an increasing sense of apprehension, maybe
even fear as we've been looking at the cost of following Jesus then,
take heart: you're in good company. Mark 10, verse 32, tells us that
the disciples themselves were amazed and afraid at this point.

But two of those disciples, the brothers James and John, seem to
be missing what Jesus is trying to explain to them. Christianity, for
them, has somehow become about personal status and reward.

Just like James and John, I too can be around Jesus, I can hear
Jesus, even see him working; I can be going to church, listening
intently to the sermons, and reading great Christian books, but if,
deep down, I am still putting myself at the centre, then God needs to
go to work on my heart today.

The reality of the disciples' hearts is revealed as Jesus is making
his third 'passion prediction' - in other words, he's predicting his
death.

Pause for a moment to feel the weight of Jesus' words in verses

33-34. Jesus knows what is coming to him. When you know the pain that's coming to you, the thought of it can easily get a hold of you. Jesus knows the pain, he describes it in verse 34, *'They're going to mock me, they're going to spit on me...'* He so easily could have lost focus in anticipation of the brutal torture and death that he was facing.

And yet, there's a tenderness here; the selfless courage and strength of Jesus, the *man*, is breathtaking.

In the face of such love and sacrifice, we might expect to see the disciples reacting with a huge, *'Wow! That's amazing!'* Maybe even falling on their faces in adoration and thanks... sadly, that's not the way it goes.

'...And James and John, the sons of Zebedee came up to him and said to him "Teacher we want you to do for us whatever we ask of you."' (v35)

I can't read that without cringing: Jesus is predicting his own, imminent death *for them*, and they're not even listening properly! They're too busy bickering over their own status.

They haven't yet learned that it's *not about them*. They probably had no idea their hearts were like this, but their mouths open and out it spills.

Gimme, Gimme, Gimme!

Their demands are rude, arrogant and childishly selfish in the worst way, and yet Jesus' response is astonishingly patient. He doesn't even get the tiniest bit annoyed with them. He simply replies, in verse 36, *"What do you want me to do for you?"*

But their shameful self-absorption isn't over yet. *"Grant us to sit, one at your right hand and one at your left, in your glory,"* they say.

It's likely they're still thinking of Jesus as a political messiah, one who will restore Israel politically from the Romans, who will literally sit on a throne and become a kind of Prime Minister. They've been thinking this through, and nurturing some political ambitions of their own.

Jesus responds, *"You do not know what you are asking."* He's trying to break it to them gently: Jesus always gives us a chance to come to our own conclusions. His rule is never a dictatorship.

You'd think by this moment, James and John might start backtracking a little, maybe show some humility: but, no. *"We are able,"* they say.

At this point, it would be completely understandable for Jesus to get angry with them to my mind, and yet, once again, his mercy flows. He's doing everything he can to keep them with him in their understanding. He says, *"The cup that I drink you will drink"*, i.e. yes, you will suffer, not to actually save the world, but you will suffer. We know from Acts 12:2 that James was the first Christian martyr, and John, the disciple who lived the longest, died in exile for his faith on the island of Patmos, so Jesus is prophesying over these disciples.

And then, in verse 40, he says something of great humility: *"To sit at my right hand or my left is not mine to grant."* This is a glimpse into the way things work with the Trinity. Jesus is telling us that he and his father are equal in divinity but have a different role. The father is in authority, and the son submits to him.

Humility radiates out of Jesus. He could have said *"Yes, I can fix that for you,"* or even *"No, I'm not going to let you."* He doesn't do that; he says simply, humbly, *"It's not up to me."*

Picture James and John standing there in this moment after they've put in their bid for glory. Verse 41 tells us: *'And when the ten heard it, they began to be indignant at James and John.'* The cancer of self obsession and pride has spread, it's no longer just in the two.

Interesting word, *indignant*. Could it be that they're annoyed that James and John got in there first?!

Mark conveys the difference between Jesus and his disciples as clearly as the contrast between light and dark. Jesus is pouring his life out in passion for them, and they respond with a list of questions about themselves, wanting only to know what's in it for them.

Jesus stands before them, speaking truth, but, again and again, the disciples do not respond well to the truth.

Press PAUSE ⑪

Take your spiritual temperature.

Ask yourself: How am I doing as I hear truth? Thinking over the last couple of chapters, how have I been responding?

When truth is communicated to me clearly, do I fully engage and strive for honesty and objectivity in my response, or do I do a 'James and John', failing to put my own ego aside to really listen and consequently miss the point?

God never tries to trick us! He's trying to be as clear as he can, because he loves us and he wants us to understand this.

Me, Me, Me

James and John had a specific problem that prevented them from understanding the things Jesus was telling them: an inability to forget about *themselves*. They're not just twisting scripture, or responding badly in general. They're putting themselves in the way of the message. For them, it's all about *me* and *my* position and *my* place.

And this is a huge hindrance for them. In verses 42-44, Jesus calls a team-talk, and says, '*Let me explain this a different way*'. He knows he's got to communicate this in a way these guys can understand, because he's putting the future of his church in their hands. Mark lays it out for us in 10:43-45:

"whoever would be great among you must be your servant, and whoever would be first among you must be slave of all. For even the Son of Man came not to be served but to serve, and to give his life as a ransom for many."

Jesus wants there to be a stark contrast between how the world operates and how the church operates. He illustrates this contrast with words that will paint the most vivid picture to his disciples: servants and slaves.

The word 'servant' here literally means 'table waiter'. We are to be table waiters! Table waiters don't get served, they *do the serving.* The fancier the restaurant, the more obvious the contrast between those who are being served and the table waiters who do the serving.

The difference between a servant and a slave is that a servant gets the job done and gets paid for it, but a slave is owned in a whole different way. As a Christian, I should feel that I'm *owned* by someone - it's a shocking concept, and not necessarily an easy one to accept.

Slaves are *owned* and *controlled* by others. Jesus doesn't want me to be someone who lives my own life as if I'm the centre, making my own decisions and directing my own destiny. He wants me to be characterised by *humility.*

The Importance Of Being Humble

Throughout the Old and New Testament, possibly the most important human quality is humility: it's the one that allows God to work with and through people.

Psalm 138:6 says, *'For though the Lord is high, he regards the lowly, but the haughty he knows from afar.'*

Charles Spurgeon famously said *'Be not proud of race, grace, face or place.'* He had a way with words! Don't let those things be what you take strength from: let humility mark you out.

The Christian preacher and theologian, Jonathan Edwards, said *'Nothing so sets you out of the clutches of the devil as humility.'*

Just imagine the impact of an army of men and women who are slaves to the call in your street, your town, in the UK, Europe, the world… what would that look like?

One thing's for sure; it wouldn't look anything like James and John's request in verses 35 and 37: "*We want you to do whatever we ask… We want to sit at your right hand and your left…*"

Just as the bible exalts humility as the sweetest of all human qualities, it's also terrifyingly clear about pride.

Idiot Proof

Proverbs 16:5 says this: *'Everyone who is arrogant in heart is an abomination to the Lord…'*

Francis Frangipane, the American minister and author, said, *'God cannot entrust his kingdom to anyone until he has been broken of pride, because pride is the armour of darkness itself.'*

But we've got to be real about this, and the reality is that there's a problem here, and that problem is me. You see, I hear these words, I believe them, and yet I can *still* make this world about *me*. Regularly.

Francis Chan gives a brilliant illustration in his book, *Crazy Love*. *'Imagine if you were an extra in a film, and for two fifths of a second, you are in a shot with hundreds of others, and the back of your head's there. Alright? Two fifths of a second of the back of your head. Imagine if you hired out a cinema, and you invited all your friends, your neighbours, your work mates, your family and you said 'Come on, you've gotta see this film, it's all about me. Come on, guys, let's get down the Odeon,' and you're all sitting there like 'This is gonna be great.' And then half way through you jump up and shout 'Did you see it? Did you see it? The back of my head there for two fifths of a second? Did you see it?'* The movie of our lives is not about us: it's about him, the Creator. We have two fifths of a second on this earth, and after our tiny moment is over, then you and I will really know it wasn't about us.

If we look from start to finish, the whole story of life is about God, God, *God. God* creates all things, *God* calls a man called Abraham, *God* sets a people free, *God* sends his son, Jesus, to earth… And here we are, in this brief moment between Jesus ascending and his return, when everyone will see clearly that it's always been and will always be *about God.*

James 4:6 tells us that God opposes the proud, which means that if I'm proud I *cut myself off* from God. Pride leads to relational breakdown because I isolate myself. Pride leads to division and disunity. Pride leads to depression when I fail, because I take myself too seriously.

Pride is something God has spoken to me about directly in the past.

I was thirty-five; a relatively young man. I was at a leaders' event in Ipswich, England, and a friend with a heart of gold and a superb ability to hear God's voice came and spoke to me. *"Tom, in the bucket of dreams that God has given you, you have picked up many of the ones that are for you personally. The next season is about allowing many of those dreams God has given to you to be experienced through your spiritual sons and daughters."*

This was clearly code for *'Time to get out of the way, buddy! I love you, I'm for you, but it's time to start to hand stuff over. Increasingly don't do the things you've always done. Instead, work hard at helping others to do them instead.'*

58

Now, this sounds all well and good, but the reality for me was much harder than that. I like preaching. I like leading. I like spotting things that need to change, forming a plan and inviting others to be part of the solution. The big danger with all this is that it can so easily and so subtly become all about you in your heart. You're the *special* problem-spotter and problem-solver. Trying to step back and let others step in was, often, agony for me. Partly because other people naturally preached differently, led differently and solved problems differently to me, but also at an even deeper level because I perceived my profile starting to decrease – and rightly so! But when you're an insecure man as I am, every fibre of your unredeemed self fights these uncomfortable feelings.

However, as the delusion that I was the centre, irreplaceable and so special started to deflate, joy began to flow once more. In fact, in the months after I handed over the eldership of the church I was with at the time, I laughed more than I had for a decade.

Please don't mis-hear me: I loved leading that church. But leadership led me to take myself, at times, very seriously. And that's when pride crept in and deluded me into a joylessness that I'd not spotted until I began to let go, with the courage from Jesus, of the roles I'd held so dear. Away from them, I'm able to embrace the Lord of glory with more energy and peace than at any time in my life. I am learning not to speak, but to listen. To participate and not to lead. To cheer on and not need to be on the stage.

How did all this change for me? Through the comfort of Christ in my soul, which far outweighs the fake and temporary comfort of feeling powerful and important. There is a joy that Jesus gives as I become part of history and no longer obsessed with my present. It is undoubtedly a death of sorts, but I can declare with all my heart that the resurrection is one hundred times more glorious! That delusion of power pales into insignificance when replaced with the purity of deep assured friendship with Jesus.

Pride can creep in when we swallow the lie of needing to be responsible for all that happens around us.

And then pride leads to jealousy, which is a real killer in our relationship with Jesus. When I believe the lie that there's not enough blessing for me, that in order for me to succeed, others cannot also succeed, I will suffer the effects.

Pride leads to churches being under-resourced, because there aren't servants available to serve. Pride leads to churches failing to pray, because only humble people pray - if you know you can't do something yourself, you pray.

Proud and Clear

In his book, *The Emotionally Healthy Church,* Peter Scazzero, a pastor of many years, has spotted telltale signs in his own life of how pride expresses itself as opposed to humility. I'd recommend reading all eighteen, but right now, let's just look at four key signs that I'm sure we can all relate to.

Scazzero found that, when we're proud, we tend to focus on the positive - the strong, successful parts of ourselves. In contrast, humility means we are aware of the weak, limited, needy parts of who we are, and freely admit failure.

If we're proud it can mean we naturally focus first on the flaws, mistakes and sins of others, whereas humility means we are aware of our own brokenness, have compassion and are slow to judge others.

Pride can express itself as we give our opinion a lot, even when not asked. The humble tend to be slow to speak and quick to listen.

The proud can be those who tend to like to control most situations, whereas the humble tend to be those who can let go and give people opportunities to earn their trust.

And reading those leaves me cringing, because I can see too many home truths here. But I mustn't lose heart and neither must you: there is hope.

Reasons to be Hopeful

Is Jesus loving, or is he cruel? He's *loving*.

Is Jesus surprised at their pride or did he know it? *He knew it.*

Jesus doesn't want to crush me or you, but, ever loving father that he is, he does want to give us a reality check. It's very easy just to stay still, but he wants us to be transformed and changed.

What I don't need is someone else telling me that if I was just better, more loving and more servant-hearted, the world would be a better place. I know that! I don't need another political organiser saying *'If you just gave everything away and served and loved each other, then everything would be better.'* I don't need someone to tell me that, I need the supernatural power required to actually *do it!*

I don't need another religious leader saying *'If you are really good and love and serve other people, then you'll change the world.'* I know that - I don't need to be told! I need power to do it!

I don't need another philosopher saying *'If you were just kinder and more loving and servant hearted towards one another the world would be a better place and everything would be ok.'* I know that! What I need is the power to do it!

Jesus has painted this picture of what he's asking of them, and where they're really at, and they're sitting there thinking *'Huh! We're doomed!'* And then Jesus says, in verse 45, *'For even the Son of Man came not to be served but to serve, and to give his life as a ransom for many'.*

Hallelujah for verse 45!

He's given us a humanly impossible thing to do: we can't do it! The world would be a better place, the world yearns for us all to be like this, whether you're a political organiser, a religious leader or a philosopher - whoever you are, we all know that this is how things should be. But only Jesus Christ can give you the solution as to *how* you do it. Only he gives you the power to do it!

God Doesn't Need Your Help

'The Son of Man came not to be served.' Let that sink in. Yes, he's asked us to be servants and slaves, but don't make the mistake of thinking that we are somehow serving him as if he needs anything. He lays that down very clearly. God does not need me to serve *on his behalf.*

Acts 17:25 says this about God: *'Nor is he served by human hands, as though he needed anything, since he himself gives to all mankind life and breath and everything.'*

There's a clue here in the phrase *'Son of Man'.* In the Old Testament, in Daniel 7:13, *'Son of Man'* meant one thing: God. It means the creator who made this planet which is at this very moment hurtling around a giant ball of fire one million times our size, at about 67,000mph, and yet we have no sense of movement. That creator is standing before them! And he's saying, *let's just be really clear - I don't need your help. I can do it!*

Many people with servants depend on them utterly - they would fall apart, without them, couldn't cope, don't know how to open a tin of beans or wash their socks - this is not the case with God.

Jesus is not putting his eggs in our basket, which is just as well when you think how scrambled we get things.

'*I didn't come to be served,*' and, if you only remember three words from this chapter, let these be them - '*... but to serve.*'

I don't know if it gets any better than that. The creator of everything is standing before them and he says *I have come here to serve you.*

Serves You Right

Do you know, Jesus serves you right now? He served you today, and he will serve you for eternity.

John Piper says this: '*God is most glorified in us when we are most satisfied in him.*'

When am I most satisfied? When I know I am being served! When I understand that God himself came, not to take from me, but to give to me, it changes everything. Remember, these words are spoken to twelve men who, even as Jesus is talking about being butchered, respond with arrogance and pride. And he covers it with grace and says *I've come here not for you to serve me and help me out because I really need it - but to serve you - to serve YOU!*

In my life, every moment of every day, I am being served by the King of Eternity. How inappropriate is that? It cannot do anything but bring glory to him. He wants me to be someone I could never be in my own strength, so that the world knows there's someone greater helping me: the King who comes to serve. The King who comes not to tell me what to do, which the whole world does - every political system, every religious system, and every philosophical system tells you what to do - he alone says, *This is the right direction, now let me serve you so that you are enabled to do it.*' It doesn't get any better, does it?

How Does God Serve Us?

He sets us free from the pride and self-obsession that has enslaved these disciples, and which enslaves us too.

He uses a phrase in verse 45, to give his life *'as a ransom'*. A ransom was the price paid for a prisoner of war, who was enslaved and couldn't free himself. Or it's the price paid for someone catastrophically in debt, who can't get themselves out. It's the price of a slave who wants to be set free but has no money.

The Son of Man serves me by paying the price for me to be set free from pride. Knowing that I can't do it myself, he came to set me free from that which I'm trapped in - my sinfulness, my self-obsession - his payment has covered it all.

All true love involves a cost, you have to give something of yourself in order to be in that relationship.

For me to be in this relationship with Jesus, I need him to give me so much more than just a bit of time or a bit of emotional energy: I need him to give me something that's going to set me free from who I am, with all my pride.

The price paid for my pride was Jesus' life. And, way back before he died, he knew that most of the time, I probably don't even think it's a big issue.

The movie is not about me. And when that truth starts to percolate my soul and I begin to repent of my pride, the most wonderful thing happens. You and I are designed to function with Jesus at our centre: that's where we find true joy, when we forget ourselves increasingly and give glory to the one who paid the ransom.

All For One, and One For All

Did he do this just for a few good, moral people who went to Sunday School? No. He did this unbelievable act *for many*. If you don't know Christ today, those words are for you. If you know that you're not a Christian but you're looking in, then let those words flood your soul with joy.

You may have done things in your life that you are ashamed of. Today, God's offering you the chance to be set free from something you may not have even realised you were enslaved to, so that you may know him intimately. At the cross, Christ was bathed in your pride and mine, and in exchange we were given freedom from that pride, and the ability to stand before God as if we had been humble all of our lives.

I'll be struggling with pride until the day I die - but because Jesus did brilliantly in the exam, I get the gift as if I passed the test.

And so, here's the twist. We started this chapter by saying *'It's not about you,'* as if it was a challenge - and it is a challenge - but we finish by saying *'It's not about you!'* And what a relief that is! Our challenge is also our solution. I'm free to live entirely, acutely aware that Christ died for me. He's the one that humbles me, changes me, pays the ransom for me; he's the spirit giver, the hope bringer - it's *ALL* about him! And so it's *really, really* not about me! When I start thinking I've got to try hard, I need to remember: it's not about me.

My job is simply to listen to Jesus' guidance, to remain attentive to his leading, and to trust and rely upon him.

It's entirely about Jesus' power.

Check Your Reality

Use this space to journal your thoughts:

How do I respond to truth when I'm confronted with it? Is it something I embrace, avoid or get angry about?

_____

_____

_____

_____

_____

_____

How do I feel about the idea of humility, and how could that manifest itself in my life?

_____

_____

_____

_____

_____

_____

What areas of my life am I prone to pride in?

_____

_____

_____

_____

_____

Try It Yourself...

❖ Pray: by its very nature, prayer is an acknowledgement of our
position under God. We approach a higher power than
ourselves, and immediately start to realign our image of our
own self-importance in line with a fresh realisation of who
we are. In The Message translation of Matthew 10:39, Jesus
says 'If you forget about yourself and look to me, you'll find
both yourself and me.' Claim this promise as you pray, ask
for God's help in forgetting yourself, and seek him earnestly.

Take It Further

Recommended reading:

The Emotionally Healthy Church by Paul Scazzero

Crazy Love by Francis Chan

Chapter Four

Mark 11: 11–25

Every Person Matters

'And [Jesus] entered Jerusalem, and went into the temple. And when he had looked around at everything, as it was already late, he went out to Bethany with the twelve.

On the following day, when they came from Bethany, he was hungry. And seeing in the distance a fig tree in leaf, he went to see if he could find anything on it. When he came to it, he found nothing but leaves, for it was not the season for figs. And he said to it, "May no one ever eat fruit from you again." And his disciples heard it.

And they came to Jerusalem. And he entered the temple and began to drive out those who sold and those who bought in the temple, and he overturned the tables of the money-changers and the seats of those who sold pigeons. And he would not allow anyone to carry anything through the temple. And he was teaching them and saying to them, "Is it not written, 'My house shall be called a house of prayer for all the nations'? But you have made it a den of robbers." And the chief priests and the scribes heard it and were seeking a way to destroy him, for they feared him, because all the crowd was astonished at his teaching. And when evening came, they went out of the city.

As they passed by in the morning, they saw the fig tree withered away to its roots. And Peter remembered and said to him, "Rabbi, look! The fig tree that you cursed has withered." And Jesus answered them, "Have faith in God. Truly I say to you, whoever says to this mountain 'Be taken up and thrown into the sea,' and does not doubt in his heart, but believes that what he says will come to pass, it will be done for him. Therefore I tell you, whatever you ask in prayer, believe that you have received it, and it will be yours. And whenever you stand praying, forgive, if you have anything against anyone, so that your Father also who is in heaven may forgive your trespasses." '

This passage follows Jesus' triumphant ride into Jerusalem. Up until this point, it's been fantastically exciting. Now, the God who designed the temple has come to have a look around it in physical person, and the silence is deafening.

'And when he had looked around at everything, as it was already late, he went out to Bethany with the twelve.' Mark 11:11

Something's not right.

The next day, Jesus wakes up and what he saw at the temple is still playing on his mind.

As they come from Bethany, Jesus is hungry: he sees a fig tree in leaf. From a distance, this fig tree looks healthy, but when Jesus goes to pick some fruit from the tree, he finds *'nothing but leaves, for it was not the season for figs.'*

We know from studying the Jewish calendar that this is happening around about March - Spring-time. When the leaves are visible, there should not have been full-blown figs, which come later in the autumn. However, there should have been what was called 'pagin' which were the beginnings of figs - mini-figs, as it were. If the leaves were there, there were always pagin, which were a popular snack to enjoy long before the full figs matured.

Jesus curses the tree, which probably looked like a bit of an over-reaction to the disciples, but he's actually still very upset about his experience the night before in the temple. When he goes back into the temple we understand that what he was doing to the fig tree was symbolic: it's not so much about the fig tree, it's all about the temple - the church.

From a distance, your church might look healthy. From a distance *you* might look *healthy*. From a distance, *I* look *healthy*.

God's Heartbeat

In verse 17, Jesus quotes Isaiah's words from about seven hundred years earlier: *'My house should be called a house of prayer for all the nations.'*

This is God's heart for the temple, a place that wasn't just busy, it was *bursting*! It was meant to be filled with people from all nations. Yes, the temple was about Israel meeting with God, we know that from the Old Testament, but what they'd missed was that it would be a place where people from different nationalities, in other words, those who weren't Jews, could connect with God.

Instead, those running the temple had become self-styled door-men at the most expensive club in town.

If you were a Gentile (that is, a non-Jew), and you were interested in this God of Israel, you knew that he was holy. You also knew you'd sinned, that is to say, fallen short of God's standards, so you brought in an animal, often a lamb, to sacrifice. God set this up as a way of demonstrating that you were serious about your sin. You brought your best animal, and you took it to a priest in the Court of Gentiles, and you expressed your desire to connect with the God of Israel by sacrificing something costly to you.

Unfortunately, the priests were systematically responding to those who came in this way by saying *That's not quite a good enough lamb, I'm so sorry! But you can buy one here that's definitely kosher, and certainly good enough. It just happens to be ten times the price of normal lambs - sorry about that!'*

The priests had also set up a sort of *bureau de change* there for people who came in from other countries with the 'wrong' coinage. But, rather than just exchanging it, they would mark it up by 25%, ensuring a tidy profit for themselves.

So, while the temple was busy, there was very clearly something profoundly wrong with it. It was like a fig tree that was beautifully leafy – it had the appearance of health - but that was actually rotten to the core, and not producing the fruit it was designed for.

This isn't just a history lesson. This passage cuts through the centuries to where I am right now. Jesus says repeatedly throughout the New Testament that the temple - a physical building in the Old Testament, is actually the 'church' - and, of course, the church is not a building, it's a group of people. I am the church. And, if you call yourself a Christian today, you are the church, too.

What would Jesus' view be if he came, physically, to you and me today? Would he say *'leaves, but no figs'*? *'Busy, but no fruit'*?

What would Jesus say if he came to your church? I've got to tell you, he's there every week, through his word and his spirit. Can you hear his voice? I can't answer that for you, but I can answer it for me:

I think he's giving me a loving kick up the backside!

Oswald Smith said '*Christians go on and on about the second coming, when most of the world hasn't heard about the first!*'

Press PAUSE ⑪

Who are you telling about Jesus?

Do you ever feel busy with church, but fruitless?

There is an issue here behind the surface problem which is obvious but very significant.

The issue is space.

There's a rule in life, isn't there, that we make space for that which we value. If you want a good body, you make space to go to the gym. If you value your rest, you prioritise and make space for your holidays. If you value your family, you'll book in dates and see them.

Do I make space for - do I *value* - those who do not know Christ yet in the way that God wants me to?

Some of you will be doing this brilliantly, praise God. And many of us haven't got this yet. We need to approach this humbly, honestly and with hearts open to God's message for us.

Before we go on, let me make one thing absolutely clear: God is *not* calling you to busy-ness. This is not a call to *do* more, and not a guilt trip. Christians are just fabulous at getting busy. Perhaps this is an invitation to do *less*, to *slow down* instead.

Spatial Awareness

There's two ways that space works: there's space externally, which we'll look at, and there's space internally, in terms of our soul and our hearts.

Externally, we see from Mark 11 that Jesus *did* something before he said something. He could have just said, *'This place is meant to be a place of prayer for all nations,'* ie this place should be crammed with those who aren't Christians, but he didn't - he started with a physical act. He demonstrated the physical, practical element. This place, the Court of Gentiles, made for those who don't know God, has become clogged up with *stuff* that the Israelites were making about themselves.

Now, I'm a simple man, and I like things simple.

God laid out the floor plan of the temple hundreds of years earlier, and it looks pretty simple to me.

This is the third Jewish temple, Herod's temple, which we're looking at in this passage. It had four sections: first of all, there was the Holy of Holies.

The second section of the temple was called the Court of Israel. This was for Jewish men.

The third section was the Court of Women, where Jewish women could come.

And, finally, there was the Court of Gentiles, which was the area for non-Jews. We can be very clear about the dimensions for the temple, which God had specified in 1 Kings 6.

So, you've got the temple itself on the left, which is 100 yards deep by 150 yards long. Then you've got the Court of Gentiles, which was 500 yards long and 350 yards wide. That's about 39 football pitches!

I think God is trying to make it as obvious as possible to the people of Israel - and to us, right now - how much space he wants to make for those who don't know him. It's massive!

Blind Spots

This challenges us today in terms of how we organise our church services. Does your church have blind spots, little things you know - where the loos are, whether to help yourself to coffee or queue for it, where to sit and when, etc - that someone coming in would struggle to navigate, and that might make visitors feel 'out of it'?

It's the basics of welcoming, isn't it? We've got to put up signs where the loos are, we've got to explain why we're doing what we're doing, we can't just make this about ourselves, because God wants space for those who don't know Christ to come and feel more than welcome; to feel that this place has been designed to enable them to meet with God.

It's the little things. Clear sign posting for people with dementia can make the difference between a great day and an awful day. Wheelchair accessibility, letting breastfeeding mothers know they are welcome. Quiet spaces for those who feel overwhelmed. The doors to church must be wide open in welcome.

And, of course, if *we* are the church, then this isn't just a physical building we're talking about. Recently, my eldest daughter, Daisy, was invited to a party. Often at parties you find that parents just drop their kids and run. Now, Daisy wanted me to stay, bless her, but I also felt the Holy Spirit say *'I also want you to stay and be here with the other dads who are staying.'* My immediate response was to say in my heart, *'But it's Saturday! I've been with people all week and I just want to be a hermit, I want to be grumpy in my shed!'*

Instead, I stayed. And, guess what? I had a great time. Nothing incredible happened, I didn't lead anyone to Christ. It was just me being myself, and the Holy Spirit within me, being friendly, talking openly, making space, sowing seeds and building bridges.

Invest and Invite

It takes the average person in the UK four years to become a Christian from the first time they meet a Christian. Many people are very cynical about church, they think it's a bit weird and wacky, so it takes years.

For many of us, the next few years are going to be about investing. This will be a season of saying, *'Lord, I'm not going to force things, I'm just going to start investing, investing, investing.'* Because actually, we can't speed this up. We can only plant seeds: God does the growing.

I must make space in my life to invest in others, to build relationships, to get to the stage with people where we're opening up to one another about the things that really matter. I cannot serve others until I understand their needs, and I cannot understand their needs until I make space to get to know them.

That's the physical space for us - our bodies are the temple - so our space must be time and place.

But there's also the issue of *heart space*.

In Mark 11:17, Jesus highlights the stark contrast between the space in God's heart for those who don't know Christ, and the lack of it in the church's heart, in Israel's heart.

'My house should be a house of prayer.'

I love those first words: *My house!* God spoke through Isaiah, and he made his thoughts pretty clear. *Who's house is this, oh Israel, oh Christians? It's mine! My house! I have particular thoughts and desires about how things are done and how things look here!*

Imagine you came home and someone had broken into your house. They hadn't stolen anything, they'd just replaced all the sofas, put their own carpets down, changed all the pictures on the walls - in a way that was utterly distasteful to you. You'd be furious, wouldn't you? *This is my house! How dare you move my stuff?!*

Hands Off!

God *owns* the church! It's his house! It is not mine or yours or the elders' or a pastor's; it doesn't belong to a vicar, deacon, canon, bishop, archbishop, priest, rector, church warden, synod or union. It is HIS! And he is crystal clear from beginning to end in his book about how it should be. He really wants his house to be a place where it is constantly expressing his huge heart-space for those who don't know Christ.

In the last chapter, we looked at Mark 10:45. Remember that last verse: *'The son of man came not to be served but to serve.'*

The son of man made space to come and to serve planet earth, to serve those who didn't know God. God's heart has always totally yearned for those who don't know him. He doesn't start loving you when you become a Christian - he loved you before he made Pluto!

The bible tells us his heart was for us *before the foundations of the earth.* God loves, adores, and wants to know your neighbours and your friends and your work colleagues. He's always been a God who has wanted to communicate this to us, even to the extent that Jesus Christ himself became the temple. Jesus said, effectively, *'if the temple is defined as the place where God meets man, this one is not working, so I will be the new temple.'* That's how much space he has in his heart for those who don't know God.

And then Jesus quotes another Old Testament prophet, Jeremiah: *'...but you have made it a den of robbers.'*

We have to understand for the Jews to make space for the nations is a big deal, because they've been bullied and intimidated for hundreds of years by many nations. When God says I want this part of your most precious thing in your whole nation to be where the nations who have treated you badly can come, I can understand why it was not easy for them to do that and they became an inward looking people.

But it doesn't excuse it.

In Mark 10:45, Jesus said we are to be servants and slaves of all for his sake. Not because God *needs* anything, but because we are called to be like Jesus, who came as a servant to the world.

A Life In Service

This means I am a servant to the people who live on my road. You're a servant to those in your road, too. You're there to wash their feet. Let that fill your heart! And even as I write it, I feel the challenge there as surely as if I was looking up at the sheer face of a mountain. But remember the next verse from that passage in Mark 10: *'For even the son of man came not to be served but to serve, and to give his life as a ransom for many.'*

He doesn't ask us to do anything that he hasn't first done for us himself. He wants our hearts to be like his heart.

There's a church in the north of England where, many years ago, the leader said, *"God, show me your eyes for this church, are we missing something?"* And he felt God say, *"Look around."* He looked round and he noticed that all the women had their purses and their handbags lying around the place, and he felt God say *"It's too safe. They think it's just their own little family get-together. I want you to be a place where the whole of your region comes."* It's not a safe dynamic. And so the pastor said to the church, we've got to change. Practically, the internal space was made, then they poured thousands of pounds into hiring buses every week to get people from the rougher estates of the area to come in - and they came in their hundreds. It went from a safe little club to a very different place.

That church is trailblazing, and it's wonderful.

But something tragic happened too. Many of the longstanding members left. They left because when it really came down to Jesus' mission, it became uncomfortable.

That's heartbreaking, isn't it? My prayer for us as the Western church is that not a single person would leave the church in this way. I think God is going to be leading us this way more and more. My deepest desire is that in the coming 5, 10, 15, 20 years, yes, God would save the lovely respectable people - he loves them too! - but that he would increasingly cause us to make space in our hearts and our lives to reach out and invest in people who will come. Church won't be a 'safe' place, but it will bring a joyful smile to the God of heaven who has always wanted it this way.

Press PAUSE ⏸

How are you doing on this in terms of the space in your life practically? The fruit doesn't come unless we make space. And this starts in our hearts, but it also then expresses itself in our timetables and in our money and in every aspect of our lives.

Facing Mountains

If you're anything like me, you might be feeling convicted, but there's a mountain of reasons in my mind as to why I'm not as Christ wants me to be. There's a mountain of fear and panic and apathy and things that, immediately, I can sense in my heart keep me from that place where Jesus wants me to be.

The most wonderful thing is we don't finish here. We come to verse 22, where Jesus, knowing the issue with these people, diagnoses it. He does heart surgery with hard-hearted people, and he offers a solution to them, and to us.

Jesus answered them, "Have faith in God." Truly, I say to you, whoever says to this mountain, "Be taken up and thrown into the sea", and does not doubt in his heart, but believes that what he says will come to pass, it will be done for him. Therefore I tell you, whatever you ask in prayer, believe that you have received it, and it will be yours. And whenever you stand praying, forgive, if you have anything against anyone, so that your Father also who is in heaven may forgive you your trespasses.'

He knows we can't solve this ourselves.

Notice that he doesn't say *'You need to do more discipleship courses, you need to hold a big special event and just try harder.'* He doesn't say that at all! It would be easier in many ways if he did, wouldn't it? But Christianity is not a chemical formula: there's no one-size-fits-all sure-fire fix in our own power here.

Instead, Jesus lifts the disciples' gaze in mercy and tender kindness like only he can, and says effectively, *You're not going to solve this with the pea-shooters of trying hard.* You need to bring out the big guns of prayer. The action he gives us is prayer, the activity is prayer, but the attitude is *faith praying*, not timid praying. It's a lifestyle where we face these mountains in our soul that stop us from being who we should be as sons and daughters of the living God. He won't let us gloss over it with a vague acknowledgement of, *'Oh, I've heard this, have faith in God - it's general advice.'* This is not general: it's specific, and it's God's gold dust to us.

Faith And Other Miracles

Praying in faith, Jesus tells us, can move mountains. And there are several mountains that I see in my soul that keep me from making space for those who don't know Christ.

The Mountains Between Us
#1 Apathy

I see it in my soul and I loathe it - am I the only one? When I think about the fact that the majority of my neighbours, my friends around this area, the mums and dads at the school gates do not know Christ in any way, shape or form… well, my apathy is horrendous, and it fills me with shame to even acknowledge it.

Oswald Smith, the Canadian pastor and missions advocate, said: *'Oh to realise that souls, precious never-dying souls are perishing all around us, going out into the blackness of darkness and despair, eternally lost, and yet to feel no anguish, shed no tears, know no travail, how little we know of the compassion of Christ.'*

If you identify even the tiniest bit with what he's saying, please, don't turn away from this issue - face it with me.

We're not meant to be like this, you and I! This is a mountain that needs to be cast into the sea. And the only way that I can move a mountain is not by trying harder, it's by saying, *God, I have faith in YOU – change me!* He doesn't tell me to have faith in myself, to try positive mental thinking, work hard, win people with wise words… No! *He tells me to have faith IN GOD!* Yes, I have this mountain of apathy, and there should be a space in here for those who don't know Christ. But by faith I make space, through prayer and fixing the eyes of my heart on God, I make space, daily, hourly, moment by moment. Apathy keeps creeping back, and I have to say No! Get back mountain! Out of my life!

I've got to go to war on it! When I feel apathy in my life, I need to understand the heart of God for this planet. That's the only remedy that will allow me to throw that mountain away, focusing on his love for those who don't know Christ, and not moving until I've had a fresh alignment, my heart with his. Pressing into him until I say, Lord, soften my soul, do something, don't let me be like the Tin Man with no heart - Lord, change me!

And then I must step out.

Because our boss, Jesus, really cares about this. When you work in an environment with a boss you quickly learn what the boss is bothered about. Is it time keeping? Then you focus on making sure you're in on time. Is it budgets? Then you make sure you get the budgets right and in on time. If it's morale, you're like, *'Hey, we're all good!'* You find out what your boss cares about, and then you focus on that.

Our boss, Jesus, he's not saying here *'I really care about fellowship'*, although he does. He's not saying *'I really care about giving'*, although he does. He's saying *'I really, really, really care about the lost.'*

And I can hear it, and never change and think that's somehow ok. But if Jesus came in here and said, *"You are a fig tree with leaf but no fruit, Tom"* - what an awful thought! I don't even want to entertain the possibility!

Jesus doesn't just say we're done for. He knows we're apathetic, and so he gives us the remedy: have faith in God. Fix the eyes of your heart on him daily. *'Let that apathy drain away as you fix the eyes of your heart on me and understand your boss really cares.'*

Ephesians 2:4 says, *'God being rich in mercy because of the great love with which he loved us even when we were dead in our sins...'*

We touched on this earlier - God's love starts for people when we were dead in our sins. When I see those around who do not know Christ, I may feel nothing, but God feels great love! *Huge* love! So much love he gave his only son. If you are reading these and you are not a Christian, but you've met Christians before and felt apathy from them towards you, can I just apologise and ask your forgiveness, because that is not representing the heart of God. God's love *burns* for you. The fact that you're reading this is not a coincidence. It is because God wildly loves you and he created you to have a relationship with him. That is why you are on planet earth, to know him, to point to him, to give glory to him, and to experience his love for you.

Understand that the mountain of apathy - which we all face - can be thrown into the sea if we pray with faith.

Mountain #2
Fear

This is a big one, isn't it?

What will they think if I talk to them and they discover I'm a Christian?

The mountain of fear is so often tied in with our own obsession with looking good and wanting others' approval. And it can be an issue of authority; I don't feel like I have any authority, I allow myself to feel intimidated by others. Increasingly, secular society seems hostile to any talk about Jesus, and I take that hostility as an attack on my authority.

But Jesus' last words to his disciples in Matthew 28:18-19 were, *'All authority on heaven and on earth has been given to me. Go therefore and make disciples of all nations…'*

These are the words of a man who has died and *come back to life*. So if you want to know someone who's got authority on planet earth, Jesus Christ is the man to look to. And in that place of resurrection, he wants to fill us with confidence! He has given you and me authority. He's proved it by defeating the grave - I can't let fear cripple me! I must say no to that mountain.

It's a daily, hourly cry of, *'God, this mountain is here, let it be cast into the sea.'* I have to fight it, and my greatest weapon is faith. At every single moment of my life, I'm a split second away from either obeying God or shrinking back in fear. Every day! The joy is that God can build in me - and wants to build in me - an ongoing faith in him so that the mountain shrinks daily, and there's more and more space for faith and confidence in Christ. That's when fear loses its grip on me.

It's understanding and believing that we don't have to make something happen: he's in control. It's not about our heroics, it's all about dependence on a grace-full God, admitting our weaknesses and acknowledging our need for his help.

I was at a gathering once and there was a guy there, and I knew him by sight from around the neighbourhood. He's a big guy and quite serious looking - a bit scary looking, to be honest. I didn't know him to speak to, but I knew that his young daughter was very, very ill. I felt a tug-of-war in my heart: *can I talk to him? I don't know him! But, Lord, I'm going to have faith in you, I'm not going to let fear govern me.* So I just went over to him. Once again, there's no great crescendo, no perfect Hollywood-style ending for me: I just went over and said *'Hi, my name's Tom, I just heard about your daughter and I wanted you to know I'm so sorry, and I'm thinking of you a lot and if there's anything I can do and -'* Since that moment, whenever I see him he honks his car horn, waves frantically... he's just opened up to me, and we've become friends. Why? Because of a single seed; I'm just planting, planting, planting, seeds all the time, not letting fear creep in. We could have remained apart, isolated: familiar strangers. But how will any of us ever communicate God's love like that?

Mountain #3
Busyness

Take two simple, world-changing steps.

First of all, review your existing time. Who are the people that you know who don't know Christ, and when can you make time to see them, text them, serve them, pray for them?

Make space, because God made space. He could have kept busy enough, sustaining the universe, but he made space to come and to give us faith in his son.

Secondly, don't just review existing time; use your time well, every day. My wife, Josie, always says, *'God can do so much with so little.'* If we just do a little bit of, *'Lord, today, wherever I am, lead me in your will...'* he would do so much, wouldn't he? With such a little amount, a tiny act of obedience, he is given permission to act – because God will never impose his will upon you. That's the whole free-will deal.

Philip Yancey quotes his pastor as saying, *'God, show me what you are doing today, and how I can be a part of it.'*

A friend of mine was in a coffee shop recently, having a little time to himself. At the table next to him, he overheard two guys talking about life and death, and it became clear that they were both atheists. He wrestled for a moment, said, *'God, no! Please, I'm just here for a little bit of time to myself!'* And he felt God say, *'Come on, have faith in me!'* And so he simply said, *'Hello, guys, sorry to interrupt -'* He introduced himself and asked if they'd heard of Alpha, and recommended it as a place to discuss faith issues. And they didn't jump up and shout *Hallelujah*! They didn't even say they might consider it. But what's important is that he was there diligently listening to what the spirit was saying, and using the time that God had given him to plant, plant, plant.

God has placed you in situations that are wonderful, unique and specific. He's not necessarily saying that you must give up your job and wander the land in search of a mission. He's saying that wherever you are, never think that busyness is a mountain that can block you from being hugely effective in his hands. Mother Theresa said, *'Never worry about numbers. Help one person at a time and always start with the person nearest you.'*

The disciples were not known for their policies, meetings or intellectual ideals, but for their acts. The longer I wait to hear God's instructions, the less clear they become, as my own fears and prejudices cloud my thinking.

Edmund Burke, the 18th century statesman, author and philosopher, said, *'The only thing necessary for the triumph of evil is for good men to do nothing.'*

I can feel short of time, but I have the same number of hours in my day as Mother Teresa and Edmund Burke. It all comes down to my willingness to let God into those 24 hours.

I have a friend called Eric, who leads a church in Canterbury, Kent. He calculated that if each member of his church led one person to Christ every three years - well, let's do the maths. There's about 400 people in our church, so let's start with 400:

In the first three years we'd go from 400 to 800.

In six years we'd go from 800 to 1600

In nine years we'd go from 1600 to 3,200

In twelve years we'd go from 3,200 to 6,400

In fifteen years we'd have 12,800 people experiencing the joy, forgiveness, liberty, healing, peace and love of Jesus for themselves – what a beautiful thing!

That's by us each leading just one person to Christ every three years and then that person doing the same, and so on.

Just imagine if all the churches across the world saw that happen. If we all had faith for one person every three years - come on, let's do this! This isn't overwhelming! This is that mustard-seed of faith that God so loves to see in us! We can see massive impact if we say God, I'm going to open up my time to you, wherever I am, whatever I'm doing.

Mountain #4
Hurt

Jesus finishes his thoughts in Mark 11: 25 with '...*and when you stand praying, forgive.*' That sounds a funny thing to end with, but the Christians that Mark's gospel was sent to were in Rome. These Christians were persecuted; they were set alight to and used as human torches. Jesus knows a huge mountain that can stop us from really being on mission can be the mountain of past hurt. He doesn't want that to happen.

It's so hard when people have hurt us. It may be family members or old friends. The idea of sharing the love of Christ with those people can make us feel physically stressed out. Jesus knows it's tough, but remember, he first forgave us. Armed with that knowledge, we need to tell the mountain of offence and resentment to jump into the sea.

When I understand that I am first and foremost, forgiven, it means that even the mountain of hurt can't stand in my way. When I realise how much grief I cause the heart of God, and yet he forgave me… there's nothing that can stop a church full of people like that; it's like a juggernaught. There's no mountain that can get in its way. If that one can really be cast into the sea, then anything can happen.

Chuck Carlson is an American pastor who works in a lot of prisons in America. He ran an 18 month discipleship programme for prisoners who had become Christians. At the end of the course, they had a big celebration where everyone would come in and celebrate the progress they had made.

There was this one guy who was in prison for killing a 20 year old girl. He'd always denied doing it, but everyone knew he was guilty. Several years into his sentence, he met Chuck, and he became a Christian, and he realised he had to tell the truth. So he did; admitted publicly to killing a 20 year old girl.

On the day of his 'graduation' celebration, he stood up and talked about Christ and how much he'd changed. There, in the crowd, was a middle aged, stately looking woman who was the mother of the daughter that he had killed. She had found out who this guy was, and she'd begged the Lord to first give her the grace to forgive him, but then she'd asked that God would forgive this man, that he would save him.

Her prayers, like arrows to the very throne room of God, yelled that she was not going to let this mountain hold her back. This was the one man on planet earth who she should least want, in an emotional sense, to become a Christian. But she knew he needed the love of Christ, and she needed a miracle to even be able to pray for him. But she prayed as a forgiven one, *'Lord, forgive him,'* and she prayed, and she prayed and - guess what? No coincidence: he became a Christian.

When he'd finished his speech, she got to her feet, went over to him, put her arm around him and she said, *'This is my adopted son.'* The murderer of her daughter! It's beyond comprehension without her deep heart-and-soul understanding of God's forgiveness for her.

That is a woman on mission! That is a woman who understood every person matters, even the murderer of her daughter. It wasn't due to her working hard on negative feelings, it's due to her saying, *'My faith is in God, my focus in life is on God, and I believe he will supernaturally transform my soul. I can't do it without him.'*

God loves us and he's not condemning us. But he wants us to be able to say as of this day, Lord, I have only a brief moment on this earth, let me be in line, emotionally and practically, with the huge space in your heart for the lost.

As we, the church, look to the future, we're going to require daily, hourly, mountain moving people. It's no surprise that the enemy hates - *hates* - an advancing church - that's why mission is hard! We've got to keep crying out: *'God, move these mountains!'*

Check Your Reality

Use this space to journal your thoughts:

Who are you talking to about Jesus? Has your faith become a 'private thing', or does it spill out naturally so that you share the gospel with others?

_____

_____

_____

If you struggle with sharing Jesus, try to work out what's holding you back - and use this as a springboard for prayer.

_____

_____

_____

_____

_____

Who are you making space for? Are all your friends Christians, or are you investing in the lives of those who don't know Christ?

_____

_____

_____

_____

_____

Write down the name of one person here who you're going to commit to praying for. Expect change – and return to this page in a few weeks' time to note any encouragements!

_____

_____

_____

_____

_____

Try it Yourself...

❖ Infuse your prayers with words of faith.

❖ Remind God of *his* promises as you pray - be specific and use the words of the bible in your prayers today, eg, Lord, according to your word, you have loved my neighbour for millennia - Lord, unveil his eyes to see you.

❖ Keep asking God to increase your faith. Dutch Sheets says in his book, Intercessory Prayer, that this is a prayer God will always answer.

❖ Keep a faith journal - a small, handy notebook that you can carry around with you and jot down answers to prayer and nudges from the Holy Spirit in. Expect to fill it!

❖ Step out in faith. Today, open your diary to God, and remain alert to the Holy Spirit's promptings. Who would he like you to talk to? Where can you plant seeds?

Take it Further

Recommended Reading:

Accidental Pharisees by Larry Osborne

Reading the biographies of other Christians can be really encouraging and inspiring. Search out stories of the lives of Mother Theresa, C.T. Studd, Hudson Taylor, Heidi Baker, Smith Wigglesworth and as many others as you can get hold of, and be inspired.

Chapter Five

Mark 12: 18-27

You Are Not In Control

'And Sadducees came to him, who say that there is no resurrection. And they asked him a question, saying, "Teacher, Moses wrote for us that if a man's brother dies and leaves a wife, but leaves no child, the man must take the widow and raise up offspring for his brother. There were seven brothers; the first took a wife, and when he died left no offspring. And the second took her, and died, leaving no offspring. And the third likewise. And the seven left no offspring. Last of all the woman also died. In the resurrection, when they rise again, whose wife will she be? For the seven had her as wife."

Jesus said to them, "Is this not the reason you are wrong, because you know neither the Scriptures, nor the power of God? For when they rise from the dead, they neither marry nor are given in marriage, but are like angels in heaven. And as for the dead being raised, have you not read in the book of Moses, in the passage about the bush, how God spoke to him, saying, 'I am the God of Abraham, and the God of Isaac, and the God of Jacob'? He is not God of the dead, but of the living. You are quite wrong.'"

The Sadducees were the leaders of the temple where Jesus had so furiously overturned the tables in Mark 11:11-25. In this passage, we see them catching up with Jesus for a 'little chat'.

On the surface they have a 'theological question' for Jesus about the resurrection and marriage, but underneath the intellectualising, there's a deeper issue: Jesus has touched a nerve, and they're feeling threatened.

These guys were the sort of people we can easily recognise today: middle class, successful with comfortable lifestyles. They were the leaders in their realm, and the scary thing is, they were *bible guys*. Their fridges would have been covered in magnets with verses on them. You know those people who, when you're scrabbling around in your brain to remember a verse, they quote it in the original Hebrew and translate it five ways before you've opened your mouth. They would have felt very at home in church - that was their territory.

So, these church leaders, who must have gone through a range of emotions, from vulnerability to indignation, since they encountered Jesus in the temple, go after him with an elaborately concocted hypothetical dilemma.

Smoke Screen Dilemmas

Mark tells us right from the beginning of the passage, the Sadducees '...*say that there is no resurrection.'* These men asking questions about the technicalities of heaven don't actually believe in life after death! And yet, here they are, face to face with Jesus, knowing that he's already

94

spoken three times about his own death and his resurrection to come. Make no mistake, these guys have been keeping a very close eye on Jesus.

They also know that Jesus has already raised a man, called Lazarus, from the dead. And they realise the implication that Jesus - *because he's God* - can speak life into humans.

So it's odd, isn't it, that these powerful men who don't believe in the resurrection of the dead, come to Jesus with this convoluted question about marriage in the afterlife? Can you imagine them getting together and working out the most complicated, confusing quandary they can come up with to try and flummox the man they're actually in full-time employment on account of? It gives you some idea of their character and how they were really feeling at this point in time: they want to make Jesus look like a fool, and they want to do it in public.

It's all about control.

When Jesus came to the temple, he took control of a place that had been under their corrupt jurisdiction. They hoped that their embarrassingly complex question would perplex or bewilder Jesus and leave him looking like an idiot, and by association, all those who were putting faith in his teaching about resurrection. That's where their hearts are at.

And that is how the vast majority of the human race operate.

Operation Cover-Up

Ever since Adam and Eve sinned against God and tried to cover the evidence, humans have been working hard at covering up truth. I have real issues, but I don't want to talk about them, so I cover them up to mask my reality.

It's something we often do unconsciously. But what we see is that God - the way, truth and life - stands in stark contrast. The world is full of truth-concealers, and God is a truth-revealer.

If you don't know Christ today, his heart is that you would know who he is, and he's so different from the rest of the world!

When I was a non-Christian, looking into the whole Christian faith, I bombarded my dad with questions about the reality of the resurrection. When I'd had the 50th book suggested to me that proved historically that it really did happen, but I continued saying *'I just need a bit longer, Dad,'* that was a smokescreen on my part. I knew that the fact was, to be a Christian would mean swallowing my pride, and admitting that for years I'd believed the wrong thing when I'd decided that Christians were crazy. It was going to be humiliating for me in front of my mates.

Maybe that's you today. Maybe you've been talking and reading about Jesus for months, maybe even years. If someone asked you about the Christian faith you might say, *'Ah, yes, I'm still seriously thinking about that…'* Perhaps you need to admit that is your smokescreen. That, really, you just need to step out. You've asked a trillion questions, it's time for a step of faith.

But it's not just when we're looking into the faith for the first time that the masking can happen. I have found that it carries on, and it's a daily battle in which I surrender to Christ or lose.

'Oh, I would get baptised, but I just have a few more theological questions. I know I've asked 5,452 of them, and I know Jesus just said repent and be baptised, but I just want to go a bit deeper, give me a bit more time!'

'Yeah, I would take up that leadership responsibility, I really would, but I'm not an extrovert like those guys out there, and I should probably become a better Christian before I stick my head above the parapet… At some point in my life

I'll do that...'

'I would start giving regularly and generously, but it's just that right now I want to sort out these theological issues about tithing...'

I can be like the Sadducees sometimes. What starts as a genuine issue can, if I allow it to trickle on rather than confront it, become a barrier between me and Christ. And in this world of concealment and camouflage, Jesus lovingly wants to get beneath the surface with me. It's uncomfortable, but it's the only way I will ever move on with Christ.

Press PAUSE ⑪

How are you doing on this?

When you hear God's truth confronting your habits and lifestyle, how do you receive it?

It's so easy to look at the Sadducees and judge them instantly as The Bad Guys, but God wants me to go deeper as I face the truth and search my heart brutally honestly.

The Sadducees didn't believe in the resurrection. They didn't believe in the reality of angels, spirits, demons or anything at all supernatural. This was their statement of belief.

This was their smokescreen. Behind it lay the issue of control.

Remote Control

They were used to being in control, those Sadducees. They were the guys that led the temple. They were the ones that told you how high to jump. They commanded their world, and mastered their own destiny.

They didn't understand that the delusion of being in control was going to kill them, this it was like a cancer that got exposed through their questions. It was a barrier between them and the kingdom of heaven.

The gospel screams at us *You are not in control!* Learning this will change your faith walk forever. If I live as if I am in control of my life, I will shut myself off from the gospel.

This is the reality: when God created Adam and Eve, there was a uniqueness about them. When he created the first humans, we see he says these words to them in Genesis 1:28.

"Be fruitful and increase in number…"

Paul Tripp in his brilliant book, Instruments In The Redeemer's Hands (published by Presbyterian and Reformed), points out that as God was creating, there's a rhythm to the literature in Genesis one: He created light, he created the water, etc, and then, suddenly, when it comes to humans, he speaks to them! He didn't talk with the rest of creation; there was no need for him to say to a tree *"Get leafy!"* or, to a crocodile *"Make it snappy!"*

But God spoke to humans, because he knew that, even though Adam and Eve were the perfect people, they were created to be *dependent.* They're the one part of creation that most displays the glory of God, but they're also the one part of creation that is most dependent on God. Not because they'd sinned, not because they were weak: simply because they were *human.* They were created to be God-hearers and God-doers, in relationship with their maker. To be naturally aware that *'God's in control and not me.'*

Our culture tends to think if I need help, it's because of something I did or something that was done to me: the result of either bad biology or bad chemistry. Genesis one tells me different. Trying to live without God is choosing to be sub-human, to live like an animal.

The realisation of a need for humble dependence was starting to dawn on the Sadducees. But the thought of letting go of their tight grip of control over their own lives and the lives of others horrified them. Their lifestyle and, perhaps surprisingly, their bible reading, had deluded them to the extent that they felt no need to be in active relationship, listening to and doing the things of God.

A Lifestyle That Lies

These guys had all the material comforts that the world affords. We looked at this in the chapter about the rich young ruler. This is the comfort delusion in full force: a lifestyle that whispers lies: *"You can be in control, you can make things happen with your own resources."*

So when Jesus came into the temple, their temple, and exerted his control, and called it *'My house,'* it turned their world upside down. And then it got worse, as Jesus began to speak about the resurrection - they've no hope of exerting control over a supernatural afterlife.

They know the power of wealth, the power of status, and the power of feeling invincible. But all this knowledge is dangerous to their spiritual health, because, as Jesus says, they don't know the power of God. This lifestyle that they're so pleased with is blinding them to the real source of power.

They're like geese sitting in a puddle, all facing the same direction, thinking they're living the dream, while behind them a reservoir shimmers in the sun.

Pick 'n' Mix Scriptures

As well as not knowing the power of God, they didn't know the Scriptures.

The bible bounced off them, and it was all about what they read, and how they read it.

The Sadducees approached the bible with a pick 'n' mix attitude, only going for the first five books of the Old Testament, the Pentateuch, written by Moses. I have a feeling that one of the reasons they liked this but didn't read the rest was that the core of the Pentateuch were the Ten Commandments.

The Ten Commandments - beautiful and true as they are - if read in isolation, can appeal to people who like to feel in control; they can think, *'Oh, I can do those.'* The other parts of scripture that are clearly supernatural, God in charge, us dependent, can freak control-freaks out.

This is why I must read the whole of scripture: the lovely bits: *Jesus is my shepherd,* and the scary bits: *Jesus is my judge.* If I pick and choose, I risk falling into the Sadducee trap.

I once heard an interview with a woman I greatly respect. But when she was asked about the difference between men and women in marriage or in church leadership, she said *'I think Paul just had it in for women, so I don't tend to read too much of his stuff'.* Now, Paul wrote huge swathes of the New Testament! But rather than humbly grappling with his words, and discovering that Paul was revolutionary in being pro-women and in promoting gender equality in a way that was unheard of at that time, she took it at face value, didn't like the sound of it and turned her back on that section of the bible.

It's so easy to become a Sadducee, isn't it? To stick to the elements of scripture that appeal to our view of how things should be, and just ignore the rest.

But it wasn't just what they turned away from; it was how they read the bits they liked: it gets worse!

Heavy Words, Lightly Thrown

In verse 26, Jesus cheekily says:

"... have you not read in the book of Moses...?"

Jesus must have had such a twinkle in his eye when he said this - everyone knew the Sadducees *were* the book of Moses! Then, with the very verse that they would have had stuck on their fridge, he delivers this beautiful paraphrase:

"... in the passage about the bush..."

He's handling them so lightly, it sounds almost casual; but here comes the hit:

"...how God spoke to him, saying, 'I am the God of Abraham, and the God of Isaac, and the God of Jacob'?..."

Abraham, Isaac and Jacob were leaders of the people of Israel, and they were all dead by the time God spoke these words to Moses. But God's saying *"I am"*, present tense.

Abraham, Isaac and Jacob are alive, is what Jesus is saying to these self-appointed religious experts. I am still their God because they are in paradise now with me. If they had been dead and no more, God would have said *"I was the God of Abraham, Isaac and Jacob..."*

The Sadducees had been pick 'n' mixing with a filter lens on - it was staring them in the face that God was a God who wouldn't be contained, dictated to or 'managed' - that the resurrection of the dead is real.

And it's in the very portion of scripture that they say they know and love.

It's so easy for me to say How can they be so foolish? *It's in the present tense, it's obvious!* But I do the exact same thing.

I say, I believe I can talk to the God of the universe, and he will actually respond - and then I hardly ever pray.

I believe that the bible tells me that if I give in a way that is generous and full of faith, it will shape my eternity in a way I can't understand - and then I don't give.

I say I believe the bible tells me that as a community, we're going to be together for eternity - and then I barely invest in relationships.

I can say I believe, as a Christian, that I am righteous before God, and that he loves me infinitely. And yet my worship can be half-hearted. I'm more distracted by a text that pings onto my mobile, or some guy who's walked in late to church, or what the person in front of me is wearing...

The issue is immaterial; the point is that I must *know* the scriptures, and live with a heart-knowledge of them daily. The scriptures must impact my everyday life, continually changing me as I grow in my understanding of them.

The Buzz Factor

My friend, Martin Segal, lead elder at The City Church, Canterbury, UK, had a picture which illustrates this perfectly. In the first Toy Story film, Buzz Lightyear starts out thinking he's invincible. He's got his little light, and he thinks it's a laser. He's got these plastic pop-out wings, and he thinks he can fly.

I can be like that if I know the world's power, and not God's. If I only know selected bits of the scriptures out of context and with my own filter of prejudice, it leads me to think that I am in control, like dear old Buzz.

There soon comes that poignant moment where he gets onto the banister, hurls himself off and plummets like a stone.

In his book, The Emotionally Healthy Church (published by Zondervan books), Peter Scazzero notices some things about himself when he's living as if he is in control of his own life:

'I'm anxious more. I'm always rushing and hurrying. My body can sometimes be in a knot. I find myself doing too many things. My mind can't stop racing. I find myself driving too fast. I'm not able to be fully present with people. I can be irritable about the simple tasks of life, like having to wait in line at the supermarket, and I'm skimming over time with God.'

Hitting The Wall

I believe God leads us to what I call 'walls'. Moments when I realise that I'm not in charge. Paul talks about it in 2 Corinthians 1:8b-10:

"...For we were so utterly burdened beyond our strength that we despaired of life itself. Indeed, we felt that we had received the sentence of death. But that was to make us rely on not ourselves, but on God who raises the dead. He delivered us from such a deadly peril, and he will deliver us. On him we have set out hope that he will deliver us again."

That's a 'wall'. It's a desperate moment for him, but in that moment, his focus is immediately on God.

Walls, uncomfortable and difficult as they are, are the kindest things that can happen to me. They're not meant to leave me in a place of despair, but to lead me ultimately to a place of worship, where I cry out to God, acknowledging his sovereignty and my dependence.

Walls take many forms: maybe you've got a new job, or got promoted, and you suddenly feel hugely inadequate to the task. Maybe you want to move house, but your house isn't selling, and nothing you're trying seems to make any difference. Maybe you've got a wayward child that you love more than life itself, but you're totally unable to control them yourself. It's the most painful feeling in the world, but it's also the kindest thing that God can allow us to feel, because that's when we'll discover that we can trust him.

He wants us to be a people who are regularly aware of 'feeling the wall' and turning to him, rather than relying on our own resources to solve all our problems.

Where I used to live, there was a well-respected non-believer, a multi-millionaire. He'd invested millions of pounds into a local community project - he was a really good, generous man. But he'd overstretched himself, and he was getting into terrible debt. He tried to sell his house; couldn't sell it. The situation got worse and worse. Just after Christmas he put a shotgun in his mouth, and for one last time he felt in control, as he took his own life.

A few months earlier things had felt very different for him. He was on the front page of the local papers, being hailed as a hero. But when he hit a wall and realised, *"I'm not in control,"* he didn't have any answer.

It's heartbreaking.

God loves us, and he wants us to learn by starting with small walls: I ask, *"Lord, what do I do now?"* and I grow in that place of dependence.

And I grow, even when there isn't a wall; that's the real trick. When there's nothing wrong, I'm still aware that I'm not managing my own life, because then I'm in a place of ongoing dependence on God.

The solution to my independent inclinations is simple, but it isn't easy. Fortunately, Jesus wants everyone to get it, not just a few learned theologians and intellectuals.

All I need to do is to know his word and his power.

But what does that mean? How do I do that, practically?

The Bible As A Mirror

Do you read the bible, or do you let the bible read you? There's a difference.

Put your hand on your heart with me: this is the place Jesus wants you to know the scriptures.

I'm in a war, and I've got to know the sword of the Spirit. If I don't, I'm a sitting target! I'll become a Sadducee without even realising it. I have to know it; I have to live it.

If I watch over four hours of telly a day, (as the average British person does according to the Broadcasters' Audience Research Board), and I get into my bible for four minutes a day - big surprise - I'm not going to fully become the person God wants me to be. I must be really practical about this. I must make time to get into the bible, and let the bible get into me.

Years ago I mentored a young man. I advised him to learn to self-feed when it came to his bible reading – it's something you have to do for yourself. He kept saying, *"Got it, got it, got it…"* But he never got round to doing any bible study. Eventually I told him that unless he actually came to the bible for himself, then I wasn't going to give him any more time. There was no point unless he was actively engaged.

He mumbled, *"Yes, sir,"* and off he went, and I thought, *"Oh dear, that was a bit harsh…"*

He came back to me the next day with three bible commentaries, and he said, *"Thank you, that was the kindest thing you've ever done for me."*

It's not rocket science, I just need to know the word. Because when I look at the word, guess what it reminds me? Yep: I am not in control.

From start to finish, it's about a God who's in control, parting red seas, calling weak people, like David, who end up having affairs and killing people, calling average-Joes to walk around a city with trumpets and see the walls come tumbling down! Again and again, God is working his purposes out through the most mixed up, unlikely people.

Even when Jesus came to earth, he didn't fight to have control; he laid down his life saying, in Luke 22:42, *"Not my will, but yours, be done."* He's the one I'm wanting to follow.

Authority Figures

Rick Warren, the American pastor and author says 'Growth comes through constant gazing upon the word, not occasional glancing.'

Who's word is it? It's God's. God's perfect, authoritative word: there it is, the 'A' word. He is in authority over us. I don't come to it and try to make it say what I think it should: I humbly submit to the word.

In the same way that Jesus said "This is my house," about the temple, scripture is also his wonderful thing. Therefore my question is not, "Lord, would this make sense if I was in control?" Frankly, the whole bible is full of things that appear not to make sense!

If I don't know his word, I will be out of sync with the God of the universe who is both incredibly loving and incredibly holy.

C.T. Studd, mentioned in chapter two, was one of the wealthiest men in England, and God spoke to him through the scriptures: "Sell everything." He knew God well enough to recognise his voice, and he gave his fortune away, and started his married life with £5.

C.T. Studd could so easily have been like a Sadducee. He had the lifestyle and the worldly power to feel really self-sufficient. He could have read his bible, given a bit of money to the poor and felt good about himself. But he let the scripture into his heart, and it changed his life forever.

The word is living and active, sharper than a two-edged sword. I need to know his word, but I also need to know his power.

The Power Through The Page

Isn't that amazing that we only know the power of God *through the page?* If I just have a desire for the spiritual things without knowing the page, I'm in a dangerous place.

Do I know God's power like a husband knows his wife? It shouldn't be a stranger to me.

People should be able to say about me, *"That Tom Shaw - he knows the power of God."* Not "Tom knows *about* the power of God." It's an intimate, close relationship. It should be part of me in the same way as my fingerprint, the colour of my skin, or the shape of my nose.

It's also a present tense relationship, never a past tense experience. God wants me to know him right now, all the time, for my whole life.

Galatians 5:25 instructs us to *"...keep in step with the spirit."*

Keep walking, keeping listening for the Spirit: it's a gentle thing: knowing the power of God requires that cultivating, that walking, that closeness with him.

When we talk about mission and personal evangelism, it's about partnership with the spirit. If I don't know that in my heart, I will feel pressure. When I'm in step with the spirit I know that he's not asking me to make something happen - *he is the evangelist!* It's great when human evangelists come, but we've got the ultimate one, the Holy Spirit, the spirit of God, and he loves the lost more than any human, and he's here right now - Hallelujah!

When I'm going to work tomorrow and I'm on the bus or train, or just walking along, he's with me and he's passionate about the lost. He's the most soft hearted evangelist ever, and he's also the most powerful one, and, best of allhe's with you right at this moment. This is not about us making things happen, it is about us keeping in step with him; listening to him; following his lead; sensing his nudge.

Jesus says it's possible to grieve the spirit. Keep an honest account: am I watching things on TV that are going to grieve him? Am I doing or saying things that will grieve him? And then am I surprised that I don't hear him?

I remember desperately trying to share the faith with my mother-in-law about two years ago. I thought I was using the best illustrations, but nothing was happening. And then I heard how she went to a farm because it was the lambing season. And the farmer, called Gerald, happens to be a man who knows the power of God. He and his family let the public in, and then they just watch as the Holy Spirit does the rest.

He went up to my mother-in-law, and he said, *"Alright there?"* She said, *"I keep coming back to this farm, I don't know why."* He said, *"It's because the Holy Spirit is here."* And after about half an hour of talking, led by the Spirit, he spoke with perfect insight into a situation in her life. In thirty minutes with a total stranger!

She went to the church that he's part of, and to cut a long story short, she became born again, and was baptised - praise God!

So here I am, the pastor in the family, and I didn't get it right! I was getting all technical, trying my hardest and he was simply led by the Spirit. On paper it looks kind of crazy and shockingly direct, but how much more powerful!

Praise God, this is available to us all, today. You might be a farmer; you might be a mum; you might be a business man; you might be 12; you might be 112: it doesn't matter! If you know Jesus, the Spirit is with you! And in this time he's trying to say - get to know me better than you know your best friend, get intimate with the word and the Spirit.

Check Your Reality

Use this space to journal your thoughts:

When I hear truth, how do I react?

_____

_____

_____

_____

_____

How do I feel about the issue of control? Spill your heart out to God, be honest about control issues in your life.

_____

_____

_____

_____

_____

What parts of my life do I struggle to give God control of and trust him with?

_____

_____

_____

_____

Try It Yourself...

❖ Take responsibility for yourself before God. Don't let anything distract you in this moment, and let his power fall on you afresh. You may want to use these words as a prayer:

> *Lord God, forgive me for the times when I try to control my world. I realise that ultimately, I can't control anything, but that you are the one in charge. Help me to surrender to your authority. Please free me from feelings of needing to control everything. Where there are 'walls' in my life, help me to turn to you for my answers. I'm so sorry for the times I haven't turned to you for help.*
>
> *Come Holy Spirit. I don't want to be a Christian who's trying really hard to work my way into the kingdom. I want to be in step with you. I want to know you. I want to hear you, moment by moment. I'm sorry for the things I've done that have grieved you. Please forgive me, and bring me ever closer to you, Amen.*

❖ Rejoice with other worshippers and invite the Holy Spirit into your life on a daily basis - seek out songs about the Spirit – and sing them regularly.

Take It Further

Recommended Reading:

The Emotionally Healthy Church by Paul Scazzero

Instruments in the Redeemers' Hands by Paul Tripp

Chapter Six

Mark 13:1-23

Reality Check – Things Are Going To Get Hairy

'And as he came out of the temple, one of his disciples said to him, "Look, Teacher, what wonderful stones and what wonderful buildings!" And Jesus said to him, "Do you see these great buildings? There will not be left here one stone upon another that will not be thrown down."'

The ice field that Captain Edward John Smith sailed the Titanic into on the 15th April 1912 would have been no surprise to him.

Other ships who were sailing in the very same waters that the Titanic was headed for sent warnings via radio. Each warning would have been logged and passed on to the officer on the bridge. Six warnings were sent on the 11th April, five more on the 12th, three on the 13th and seven on the 14th, the day before the 'unsinkable' ship

111

went down, taking over 2,220 people to an icy grave.

If you put all that we've covered so far into place – praying for faith, stepping out in that faith, depending on God, being intentional and disciplined in developing your relationship with him - even then - to follow Christ means that a metaphorical ice field lies ahead of you.

Ignoring warnings is dangerous and foolish, and Mark 13 is one such warning for Christians. Unlike the captain and officers of the Titanic, you and I must not ignore these warnings.

Here Comes Trouble

And so this passage begins with Jesus telling the disciples that the temple - a building considered as indestructible as the Titanic was unsinkable - would one day fall. Imagine going for a stroll in London with someone who, as you walk past the houses of Parliament, says, *"That's all going to come tumbling down."* You might manage to keep your face composed, but inside, you'd be freaking out, wouldn't you? Not because of the idea that the prophecy might be true, but because you'd be wondering about the sort of person you were hanging around with.

Jesus knows what the disciples are feeling, so, from verse 3, he explains more fully:

'…As he sat on the Mount of Olives opposite the temple, Peter and James and John and Andrew asked him privately, "Tell us, when will these things be, and what will be the sign when all these things are about to be accomplished?" And Jesus began to say to them, "See that no one leads you astray. Many will come in my name, saying, 'I am he!' and they will lead many astray. And when you hear of wars and rumours of wars, do not be alarmed. This must take place, but the end is not yet. For nation will rise against nation, and kingdom against kingdom. There will be earthquakes in various places; there will be famines.

These are but the beginnings of the birth pains.

"But be on your guard. For they will deliver you over to councils, and you will be beaten in synagogues, and you will stand before governors and kings for my sake, to bear witness before them. And the gospel must first be proclaimed to all nations. And when they bring you to trial and deliver you over, do not be anxious beforehand what you are to say, but say whatever is given you in that hour, for it is not you who speak, but the Holy Spirit. And brother will deliver brother over to death, and the father his child, and children will rise against parents and have them put to death. And you will be hated by all for my name's sake. But the one who endures to the end will be saved.'"

In the first thirteen verses, Jesus describes what I call trouble with a small 't'. Not that the trouble is insignificant or easy, rather that it is specific, and localised.

And Jesus is right. Over the next 40 years, from AD30 - AD70, these men listening to him would experience real suffering. We see in the book of Acts that there is great church growth, but also great persecution. In AD70, Herod the Great's temple, which took more than eighty years of his reign as emperor to build, which was clad in pure gold with tips of white stone, and which was believed to be just as indestructible as the Titanic, did indeed become a pile of rubble.

Jesus knows exactly what the future holds, and he's warning his followers that there will be a specific backlash as a result their allegiance to him.

The disciples listening to him would, in the coming years, form the leadership of the first 'mega-church'. Later on, one of them, Peter, speaks a very 'normal' sermon – by which I mean no special effects, no drama presentation, no surprise miracles - but through the power of the Holy Spirit, 3,000 people respond. (See Acts 2:38-41 for the full story). It's wonderful! We all want to see that, right?

But with the excitement of seeing such growth and people influencing their culture because they get saved, we also see increasing hostility, persecution, and a rise of Jesus-haters. The two come together: church growth and opposition.

Jesus is warning them - and us - to expect problems, and, more than that, he's saying it will be normal for us to encounter such difficulties, because trouble is our trademark.

Great Expectations

All throughout the New Testament you see this recurring dynamic. Acts 1-7 is all about growth. Acts chapter 8, persecution comes: it's all about expectations.

When Josie and I were first married, one of the biggest learning curves was expectations. My expectation of a day off is that I do absolutely nothing: my dynamo of a wife has different ideas. My expectation of a holiday is that I do... absolutely nothing; let's just say Josie approaches things differently.

Jesus wants us to get our expectations right. We'll see amazing things happen, but we'll also see trouble: specific, localised strife in response to a growing church.

Acts 17:6 talks about the religious leaders from Thessalonica, describing the Christians who are coming, saying, *These men who have turned the world upside down have come here also...'*

That's the bible showing us how the early Christians were known: as people who turned the world upside down! Jesus Christ was taken to the cross because he turned the world upside down. Stirring things up should be part of a Christian's DNA.

Is it part of yours?

The Reverend Tom Wright, bishop, scholar and writer, tweeted that, *"When Paul went to a city, he caused riots. When I go to a city, we drink tea."*

If nothing's wrong, it's probably a sign that something's not right, and Tom Wright sees that, he's put his finger on something that's so easy to miss as we get derailed by the comfort delusion.

Many of us want the approval of others so much that just a frown from someone at work can put us off talking about Christ. Have you ever had the experience where you're friendly with someone, and then you just go for it, and try to communicate something about Christ and the church, and the relationship goes from friendly to frosty?

I hate that - but it's biblical! We cannot be authentic without some people saying, *"You're the fragrance of life,"* as it says in 2 Corinthians 2:14, and other people saying, *"You stink!"*

It's all too easy to be odourless, and that's what Tom Wright's getting at. Causing a ruckus should be the normal course for the church.

Just look at verse 13 of Mark 13:

"...you will be hated by all for my name's sake..."

Was it just a one-off thing that they were going to live in a really bad time, and for us it would be different? Unfortunately, I don't think so. It's harsh! If you're from a family that doesn't follow Jesus it means there will be times when your values may well clash with your parents' values. And that's so hard, but if you're being obedient to Christ, it's biblical. Why do we find it easier to offend God than our parents? We need to learn that trouble – turning things upside down - when you're obeying Christ, is actually a sign that you're doing something right.

So, when a Devonshire County Council open their meetings with prayers, the secular society takes them to court to try to get the practice banned.

Christianity is offensive, and the bible says that's when it's most likely to be authentic.

105,000 Christians will die this year because of their faith: on average, a Christian is killed every five minutes because of their beliefs. They could easily not be martyred; all they'd have to do is not stand up for Jesus. They could just keep quiet and not upset anyone. Then they'd live. But they've understood something about God that we all need to grasp for ourselves.

Costly Christianity

For some of you, following Christ will be really costly. To say otherwise would be to lie to you or patronise you. The bible lays it out really clearly. Jesus loves us utterly, and he doesn't want us to be unprepared. If your expectations are that becoming a Christian is a sweet, sugary thing, you need to adjust your thinking. It's messy, painful, difficult and gritty, and Jesus doesn't want us to be under any illusions, he's warning us from the outset.

But the trouble widens in scope, as Jesus continues in verse 14:

But when you see the abomination of desolation standing where he ought not to be (let the reader understand), then let those who are in Judea flee to the mountains. Let the one who is on the housetop not go down, nor enter his house, to take anything out, and let the one who is in the field not turn back to take his cloak. And alas for women who are pregnant and for those who are nursing infants in those days! Pray that it may not happen in winter. For in those days there will be such tribulation as has not been from the beginning of the creation that God created until now, and never will be. And if the Lord had not cut short

116

the days, no human being would be saved. But for the sake of the elect, whom he chose, he shortened the days. And then if anyone says to you, 'Look, here is the Christ!' or, 'Look, there he is!' do not believe it. For false christs and false prophets will arise and perform signs and wonders, to lead astray, if possible, the elect. But be on guard; I have told you all things beforehand.'

This is what's called a 'double-reference', a double prediction. Jesus is predicting both the end of the temple, but he's also giving a picture of the end time distress that Christians will face; it will be global and general, and no one will escape it. This is Trouble with a capital 'T'.

And the reason for all this trouble is that the gospel is, in its very essence, confrontational. It's good news, but it's confrontational, because to present the gospel is to say to others, *'When you think that you are at the centre and God isn't real, you're wrong.'* People can get very defensive in response to this idea. It takes a miracle to turn someone's heart to Christ.

I remember onetime when I was chatting with my neighbour in the street I used to live in, and he was talking about some religious people in the street. He was saying, *"They are such hypocrites!"*, and I have to admit that, in large measure, I agreed - I didn't say so, but I felt he was probably right. But then I had this jolt, this reminder of God's truth, and I had to say, *"Yeah, but you're a hypocrite, and I'm a hypocrite too!"* The bible says it's not just them - it's all of us. At that moment it went from being friendly banter to being somewhat frosty. One minute we're chummy, but then the gospel came in, and the gospel tells us we're in all the same boat, sin-wise. The gospel can take us from friendly to frosty in a flash. It's unpleasant and difficult, cringey even - I've got to live next to this guy, and I also want to be obedient to God; I find myself in conflict at that moment: it sure felt like the temperature between us dropped.

God is not just powerful, he's also moral, and that's what the world hates: that God loves some things and he hates others. The more you say, *"Lord, I want to live to please you, love the things you love, hate the things you hate,"* the more evident it will be that you are someone who is not on the same team that you once were. Your values will be different to the world around you. You're like a Manchester United fan who's been seated at the Manchester City end of the football stadium: you stand out.

Yes, Jesus is peace and love, and we seek these qualities wholeheartedly. But even in our best efforts to do that, Jesus says there will be trouble.

Keep Looking Up

At this point we need to lift our gaze:

'These are but the beginnings of the birth pains.'

The more you dwell on this verse, the more the whole thing links together. Birth pains hurt! I can speak only as a witness to them, but I've seen first-hand that they're bad.

And yet, they're not a sign that something's wrong.

In fact, they're a sign that something good is happening, and something glorious is going to come. All these things Jesus is predicting, all this trouble and strife, it's painful, but it's not a sign that something is wrong. It's a sign that something very, very good is going to come.

Ultimately the glory will be the return of Jesus Christ and the restoring of all things to be new, but there's more here - the birthing of real authentic church; churches get born through this refining pain.

Real, robust Christianity gets born through this persecution and strife.

But we should note that calling them birth pains doesn't mean the second coming is going to happen soon.

For my wife, Josie, the length of time between her waters breaking and the birth pains occurring and Daisy, our eldest, being born, took 48 hours. That's a long time to have those kind of pains! Some of you have maybe had longer, but believe me, it went *on and on*! So there's no timescale provided here - that was never part of the deal. The deal is that we must expect pain, but it's a kind of good pain, because something glorious is going to happen.

Pack Your Bags

First time dads are terrified. I was. It's week 39, this baby might decide it's coming at any moment: have you done everything you can to be ready? You've got your neighbours on red alert, you've told your parents. But there's also the ultimate issue of *The Bag*. It's in all the magazines: *Have you got The Bag ready, with 15 toothbrushes and 45 flannels and 62 bars of soap? HAVE YOU GOT THE BAG READY?!*

Everyday, you check the bag: is it ready? Yes, it's ready. Are you sure it's ready? Yes, I think it's ready, I'll just check it again...

When the time comes, there it is, checked and re-packed a hundred times, with everything you need.

Jesus is giving us a chance to pack our bag, and be ready. He didn't just say, *"It's going to happen, so, good luck - byeeee!"*

He gives us 19 imperatives in Mark 13, and you can condense them down to the following few.

Firstly, anxiety. He reassures us repeatedly, *Don't be alarmed, don't be anxious, don't be scared*. I love this, because, let's face it, we're all

119

freaked out by what we've read here, and Jesus knows that. He smiles and says, *take a breath, take courage.*

Fear can rob a church of what God wants for it, and many Christians are the biggest panickers on planet earth! We're not allowed to be, alright?! It's in the bible: we really don't need to panic.

Jesus wouldn't tell you to do something if he wasn't going to enable you to do it. I can often think, *'I'm a worry-box, that's just the way I am.'* No, it's not. If I know Jesus I am a brand new creation in God, and he wants to fill me with an amazing power to resist anxiety. We need an attitude of dependence and resultant security, followed by actively avoiding being led astray.

Jesus talks repeatedly about men who will try and lead us astray. Gifted, anointed leaders, who can really preach and who are inspirational, but whose character is rotten, and who want to lead us astray. And, unfortunately, when we're facing trouble we're more vulnerable to being led astray.

In recent years, we've seen many gifted speakers who have started tweaking and twisting the details of Christianity to make it gentler, more appealing and less challenging. And some people are swallowing it, because often these communicators are, quite simply, really cool! But Jesus warns us - don't be led astray by these twisters, because they're peddling empty promises. Don't fill your bag with stuff that won't help you.

Instead, be on guard. Guard your heart with all vigilance, as Proverbs 4:23 says. Whether you're a man, woman, old or young, guard your heart and your mind, particularly as Christ will return at any given moment, like a thief in the night.

Preach, Pray and Press On

Verse 10 tells us that when trouble comes, we are to preach. Perhaps not the answer we would expect to hard times, but we're told that the gospel must be proclaimed to all nations, and that we are to do so unashamedly. It doesn't mean I should scream at people, it means there is a boldness, a deep-down confidence. I don't try and woo people, I simply proclaim the gospel. Note it also doesn't say, *'If you're a preacher / vicar / pastor / evangelist / missionary'* – this is for all of us.

It's funny, isn't it, how, faced with having to present the gospel, we can suddenly panic as if we're not entirely sure what it is. As if we were trying to explain the internet to a cat, we complicate it in our minds.

So, what's the gospel? It's the good news that only Jesus is the one who can ultimately deliver us from trouble. He has defeated sin, he has defeated death and he has proved it by rising from the dead, and he wants to give us a chance to know him.

That's it! It's not about using fluid and persuasive words. You might be a pastor or a plumber, a cook or a criminal, a landlord or a lawyer. You don't need to have ever stood up at the front of church. You might be a mum who mainly proclaims the gospel to your children. You might be housebound, proclaiming it to social services' visitors. You might be in prison, proclaiming it to inmates and guards. We're *all* called to be proclaimers. It's not about standing up in church, it's about speaking out wherever you are, right now.

I remember when I was an atheist, at university. I was walking past a bar on campus one evening, and I saw a girl I knew a little. I said, *"Hi, Suzy, been having a beer?"* And she replied, *"No, I've been praying."* It wasn't just the fact that she said 'praying', it was the way she said it: she preached it, boldly. She didn't scream it, but it

121

challenged me, and the moment went from friendly to frosty. I narrowed my eyes and said, *"Don't you try and convert me, I probably know more than you do,"* in my shameful arrogance. But the seed was sown, and the rest, for me, became my history, and will be my destiny.

It's not about having great style, it's about being real, honest and unashamed. God wants his church to be international in its scope, proclaiming, not *whispering*, the gospel.

The Key of Prayer

And then in verse 34, we're told to pray. *Pray, pray, pray* - it comes up again and again and again, doesn't it?

William Spurgeon said, *"Anything is a blessing which makes us pray."*

So, you've lost your job, you've split up with your boyfriend or girlfriend, your housemates are a nightmare, your marriage is hard work, you're single and wishing you weren't, your mum or dad is really sick… whatever it might be, the bible says ultimately is a blessing, because it pushes you to pray, and prayer draws you into an active relationship with God.

Now, that's definitely easier to say than to feel, and I don't want to be glib about this. Once again, I'm reminded that Jesus never said it would be easy, but he also promised to be with us right in the midst of the trials of life, through pain and suffering, he never leaves us.

D.L Moody, the great preacher, said, *"I'd rather be able to pray than to be a great preacher; Jesus Christ never taught his disciples how to preach, but only how to pray."*

He wasn't diminishing preaching, but if he had to choose, he'd rather be the world's best pray-er.

We must persist in prayer, and our prayer needs to be about being strong, rather than about being safe.

In the house we lived in for our kids' early years, every time Josie took Daisy, Lily and Poppy to school and nursery, she had to negotiate a long, horribly busy, fast road. It was so scary, and I prayed every time they walked out of the door, *'God, keep them safe!'* It's not a bad prayer, but I felt God say to me one time, *'You can't just stop at safety, pray for their souls, because there will come a time when they, like everyone, will die.'* So now, my biggest prayer is, *'Lord, let them know you and let them stay strong in you.'* I can't just pray for safety, as much as I long for it. I must pray for their souls, that they will be strong when trouble comes.

The Rewards Of Endurance

Finally, we press on, as *'those that endure to the end'.*

We must develop an enduring spirit. John L. Mason says in his book, An Enemy Called Average (published by Insight International Inc), *'I believe that when God sees someone who does not quit, he looks down and says, "There is someone I can use"... Quitting is the only decision we can make that can keep us from reaching God's goals in our lives.'*

J.C. Ryle, a great clergyman who lived in the 1800s, understood this. It was said of him that he was *'a man of granite, with the heart of a child'.* He married Matilda in 1845. Within the first two years of their marriage, they had a daughter, and then Matilda was taken ill and died. Three years later, he remarried, this time to Jessie. They had four children together, but within six months of the marriage, Jessie became ill, and remained so for the next decade, at which point, she also died. No wife, five kids, busy church: he kept on going, believing God. He married for a third time, and this time his wife lived a long, healthy life, and helped care for his children.

However, in those days, the Church of England was rife with

liberalism, and was disregarding the bible entirely. He was a lone voice who believed the bible was true, and he experienced great persecution as a result. The ridicule and aggression against him was strong, but he said, *"I made up my mind to not give a jot what people said about me, but only live to please my Lord."*

Don't you want to be like that? If we want to see growth, we'll also see trouble. But the trouble must not cause us to be anxious; it's simply an inevitability, part of our obedience to God.

Trouble is our trademark. And when that occurs, the issue is not safety, retrieval, hibernation or holding on: it's staying strong, preaching, praying, and pressing on in the things of God.

Strength to Strength

If we stopped at this point, we might be in danger of sounding like most religions in the world, urging each other to try ever harder.

But Christianity is not about *trying* hard; it's about *trusting* God.

Jesus is real about the trouble, he's honest about how we need to respond when we find ourselves in it, but he also gives us the power for the impossible.

We glimpse it first in verse 11:

"And when they bring you to trial and deliver you over, do not be anxious beforehand what you are to say, but say whatever is given you in that hour, for it's not you who speak, but the Holy Spirit."

When people respond badly when you try and talk about Christ, the Holy Spirit will be with you in a heightened way at those moments.

Many of us Christians, when we think about knowing the nearness of God, say, *"Let's have another prayer meeting."* Don't get me wrong, I love prayer meetings! But actually, radical mission, where you feel very, very vulnerable is the place where Jesus' presence will come upon you in an incredibly powerful way, and he will give you words that astound you.

It's not always about gathering to pray, although, of course, that is massive and vital.

Many of us today love God, read the bible, serve in church, pray, give, and so on, but feel that there's something missing... It's because we're not actually on mission.

Press PAUSE ⑪

How are you doing on this?

Are you in a place where you're vulnerably stepping out, where it could all go wrong? Because Jesus is in those moments. As you step out, scary as it is, he promises the Holy Spirit to you. It's an ingredient that sometimes we miss, because we're so, so nervous about facing disapproval. God wants to lift us and focus our fretful eyes with a promise that if we'll step out, he'll step out with us. He'll give us the power to overcome anxiety, to resist being led astray, to stay on guard, to preach, to pray, and, ultimately, to press on.

One Day

And, finally, we have an awesome promise in verse 24-27:

'But in those days, after that tribulation, the sun will be darkened, and the moon will not give its light, and the stars will be falling from heaven, and the powers in the heavens will be shaken. And then they will see the Son of Man coming in clouds with great power and glory. And then he will send out the angels and gather his elect from the four winds, from the ends of the earth to the ends of heaven.'

It's not just about knowing the Spirit in the moment, it's about knowing the Son in that moment. That great moment that every Christian should be living for! We don't talk about it much, do we?

One day, Jesus promises that the trumpet will sound, and he will return, and all the people who've been pretending to be the Messiah will be exposed as the liars that they are, and the world will see the truth beyond a shadow of a doubt.

The imagery here of the sun darkened, and the stars falling portrays a cosmic collapse. All those who, for centuries, have put their faith and trust in the stars to guide their destinies or explain our existence in some way, will watch them fall. That's going to be horrendous for those poor people! Instead, rising up in glorious, indestructible power will be the Son of Man riding on clouds of glory.

Here's the urgency of our message: people must know the facts in order to make their decisions. God created free will for humans, and he never forces us to worship him, or even acknowledge him. But I don't want any of my friends or family to watch those stars fall and wonder why I never passed on the warning to them.

Finally, Jesus tells us he will *gather his elect*. Throughout the Old Testament and the New, scattering is a sign of things going wrong, a sign of God's displeasure. Now, it's a time for gathering. That's why the gathered church is the beginning of God's new order. It doesn't say *'gather the religious,'* and neither does is say *'gather those who have done really well and tried really hard.'* He calls you his *'elected one':* do you feel the warmth? He has chosen you.

Not because of anything you or I have ever done, just because he loves you. If you are not a Christian today, and you think following Jesus is about somehow earning your way to heaven, this passage is screaming a big 'NO!' at you. It's about his grace, it's about his mercy. He loved you first, before he created the world, you were precious in his sight; worth dying for.

So, we mustn't put our hope in this world, great as it is – and believe me, I love the comforts this world offers! Instead, we must put our hope in the world to come. Live for that world: put your investments there, your time, your energy, your money, focus it all there, because that is the one true place. This brief life we have here will be like the blink of an eye.

And, if you're still not convinced about Christ, my one huge appeal to you is that you look into the resurrection of Jesus, because if someone really has died and come back from the dead, that is the most important thing you can ever know. And if Jesus Christ really did rise from the dead, and then appear to hundreds, as the bible tells us - then the idea of him returning is not impossible to believe at all.

Let the day that's coming be a day of great celebration for you, where God looks upon you and says, *"I look at my Son's goodness at the cross, and I credit your account with all of his obedience."*

Check Your Reality

Use this space to journal your thoughts:

How do I feel when I think about stepping out to speak about Christ in my daily life?

_____

_____

_____

_____

_____

What barriers rise up in my mind that hold me back?

_____

_____

_____

_____

_____

_____

What opportunities do I have or what situations am I in where I could step out?

_____

_____

_____

_____

_____

What promises of God do I need to hold on to right now?

_____

_____

_____

_____

_____

Try It Yourself...

❖ Pray - we keep coming back to it - because it's so essential and central to Christianity. The central point of Christianity is a real relationship with the creator of the universe - and relationships don't happen without some measure of talking and listening going on. Pray ahead of any suffering you may experience, that you will remain steadfast in Christ. Ask that God will strengthen you at all times in your life, both good and bad.

Take It Further

Recommended reading:

Red Moon Rising: The Story of 24/7 Prayer by Pete Greig and Dave Roberts, Kingsway Publications

Prayer: Experiencing Awe and Intimacy with God by Timothy Keller, Hodder Paperbacks

The Grace Outpouring: Becoming a People of Blessing by Roy Godwin and Dave Roberts, David. C. Cook publications

There are many, many more books on prayer – ask friends for recommendations, trawl bookshops and pray that God will lead you to the right volume so that you fill your mind with the very words he has for you!

Chapter Seven

Mark 14:1-9

So Near, Yet So Far

Proximity and intimacy are two very different things. In this chapter of stark contrasts, we'll explore how you can be someone who is in the proximity of Jesus and yet have no intimacy with him at all. We begin this chapter by looking at an act of intimate adoration; later we'll look at how difficult that can be for us, and how we can approach that challenge realistically in order to really live in an ongoing, authentic relationship with Jesus Christ.

It was now two days before the Passover and the Feast of Unleavened Bread. And the chief priests and the scribes were seeking how to arrest him by stealth and kill him, for they said, "Not during the feast, lest there be an uproar from the people."

And while he was at Bethany in the house of Simon the leper, as he was reclining at table, a woman came with an alabaster flask of ointment of pure nard, very costly, and she broke the flask and poured it over his head. There were some who said to themselves indignantly, "Why was the ointment wasted like that? For this ointment could have been sold for more than three hundred denarii and given to the poor." And they scolded her. But Jesus said, "Leave her alone. Why do you trouble her? She has done a beautiful thing to me. For you always have the poor with you, and whenever you want, you can do good for them. But you will not always have me. She has done what she could; she has anointed my body beforehand for burial. And truly, I say to you, wherever the gospel is proclaimed in the whole world, what she has done will be told in memory of her.'

Familiar Strangers

In previous chapters, we've seen the rich young ruler, who was close to Jesus physically, and yet tragically, because of his love of money, struggled to become intimate with Jesus.

We've looked at the Sadducees, who knew parts of the bible inside out, and yet, despite their physical proximity to Jesus, they were a million miles away from him on a heart-level.

Now we see that even the disciples, who could say absolutely that they were near to Jesus *physically*, were so far from him in terms of *intimacy* at this moment in time.

There are plenty who will follow Jesus in the crowd, but very few who will follow him to the cross. I might grow up in a Christian family and be around the teachings of Jesus all my life, attending church and doing all the 'stuff' of Christianity, and yet I can entirely miss out on a deep, personal, heart and soul familiarity with Christ — the very nature of the relationship he calls me to, and longs to share with me.

Emotionally Involved

Did you spot the difference in response between the men in the story that we've just read and the woman?

Cast your mind's eye over the scene; we don't know much about Simon the leper, but one thing is clear - he had leprosy at some point in his life, and it seems likely that he has now been healed. Leprosy wasn't just a terrible physical condition, it also meant social exclusion. In those days if you got leprosy, you were rejected from your community.

In my own life, from the age of 11 to 18, I had very bad skin. Obviously, it was nothing compared to leprosy, but for me, those years were very painful, and I was crushed by feelings of self-consciousness and inadequacy. No one rejected me in an obvious way, and yet my awareness of my condition meant that it dominated every waking moment for me during those years. In my mind, it defined me, and I felt miserable. Multiply my experience by about a million, and you might be able to imagine a little of what Simon the leper would have gone through: not just a physical condition, but crushing social rejection and a deep personal awareness of his physical condition and its effect on those around him.

Wonderfully, this social outcast is now playing host to the Son of God and his disciples. It appears he has been healed, and embraced, socially.

Across the room, we see someone else, actually not mentioned here, but mentioned in the other account, in John's gospel, chapter 12. It's a guy called Lazarus. He wasn't someone who had leprosy and was healed: he was someone who had *died*. He physically died, was buried by his sisters, Mary and Martha, and was raised to life by Jesus.

So we have an ex-leper and an ex-corpse sharing an evening of food and company with their saviour, and then along comes this woman with her loving act of anointing Jesus' head with expensive perfume. And the emotional response of these two men who owed so much to Jesus is… apparently nothing.

The disciples were there, too. They may not have had leprosy or been raised from the dead, but they could certainly have said that being with Jesus had been life changing for them.

And yet, according to scripture, their emotional warmth towards Jesus doesn't even merit a mention.

In stunning contrast, consider the response of Mary to her Lord:

'[she]…came with an alabaster flask of ointment of pure nard, very costly, and she broke the flask and poured it over his head.'

This might sounds a bit odd to us in western culture today, but it's a costly and symbolically significant thing that she's doing here. Nard was a perfume associated with burial, and the disciples tell us it was worth 300 denarii: that translates as the equivalent to about a year's salary. So, in today's terms, £25,000 - £30,000 pounds worth of perfume was contained in the flask that she broke.

Smashing it is a moment of utter adoration and deep emotional response. There's no doubt this woman is emotionally alive to Christ here while, in contrast, the men appear emotionally numb.

Reactive Substance

Let's clear up a few points concerning this woman before we go any further.

She knew the cost of that nard just as well as the men did. She was not acting in ignorance. It was not a mistake or an oversight upon her part, or foolish economy. It was a deliberately extravagant act in response to a deep state of gratitude on her part.

The woman is not named in the gospel account. Some theologians feel it was Mary, Martha and Lazarus' sister, who famously sat in rapt attention when Jesus visited their home on another occasion. Others believe it was Mary Magdalene, the ex-prostitute whom Jesus had freed from the life of shame and hurt that had trapped her. It's quite likely that it was a different woman – Jesus had lots of female friends and followers. In a society that oppressed and dismissed women, he treated them with dignity and respect, raising them to equal standing with the men around him. His revolutionary attitude towards them won him their loyalty and adoration – as we see in this extraordinary gesture.

We'll call the woman Mary, for clarity and simplicity, although she is not named in the passage. We won't get bogged down by a discussion of her DNA here; it is her emotional response to Jesus that I want us to learn from, not her genetic identity.

The first thing that we can learn from Mary is that she was not afraid to make herself vulnerable in front of others to demonstrate her love for Jesus. She opened herself up to criticism because, for her, it mattered more that Jesus knew how much she loved him than it mattered what others thought of her.

Press PAUSE ⑪

Where are you in this picture?

Do you identify with Mary, or with the men?

Do you let your emotions get involved in your relationship with Christ, or is your faith expressed through a stiff upper lip? How do you feel when others around you grow emotional in times of prayer or worship? When someone brings a word during a service and they get passionate in delivering it, how's your heart reacting? When you feel moved to an emotional response of your own do you let it out, or swallow it down until you have regained control of yourself?

I can be spiritually in a fairly good place, reading my bible, knowing it quite well, attending church and small group, giving money to the church, and looking just fine, while, in reality, I am emotionally entirely switched off.

We, the church, can be guilty of boxing up life, drawing imaginary lines between the 'spiritual stuff' and everything else. These lines were never drawn by our creator. Humans are not just spiritual beings: they are physical and emotional, and that is how God made us. What we're seeing here is a woman whose emotions are alive in a way that makes Christ say, '...*wherever the gospel is proclaimed in the whole world, what she has done will be told in memory of her.*'

In contrast to the dignified dullness of the blokes it is extravagant, ridiculous, irresponsible emotion expressed through a particular action. The action is actually secondary; it's the state of her heart that pleases Jesus so much.

We can also fall into the trap of trusting the intellectual over the emotional, and valuing knowledge and study above a heart-felt gut response to Christ. In the same way that our education system holds subjects like maths and science at the top of the value-tree, while (wrongly) placing drama and dance as add-ons somewhere far below, we can put theological knowledge and 'serious' study on a pedestal, while de-valuing the simple act of dancing for joy at the realisation of God's love for us, or weeping heartfelt tears of repentance in the acknowledgement of our own sin.

Our constant need is to engage ourselves fully – intellectually and emotionally – in our search for God and our response to him.

At this point, it's tempting to let myself off the hook by telling myself that her response says more about her general temperament than anything else. I can say that this woman may be naturally one to lose herself in the moment, regardless of those around her. I can say she's a risk-taker, impulsive and inclined to excess. Neither of these lines of thought really challenges or helps me to understand my own response to Jesus, though. This way of thinking is a red herring.

It doesn't matter if you're an introvert or an extrovert, if your hand gets in a car door and someone slams that door, believe me, you're going to have a response. The degree to which I respond to something is not just about my personality; it's to do with the magnitude of the *cause* of what I'm feeling.

It's God's passion that you would know Christ and have a life of profound, God-purposed emotion. He doesn't want you to be ticking lots of 'Christian' boxes, and yet be totally numb towards him emotionally.

Wasted Emotions

There is a moment in this passage when these men do come alive emotionally – did you spot it? It's in their response to the cost of the perfume. It's a smokescreen when they say the money should be given to the poor; the reality is, they hate the idea of money being wasted, and they view Mary's actions as wasteful. That's why Judas, in the coming verses, begins his betrayal of Jesus to get the silver: his true god was exposed as he watched £25,000 being poured over Jesus' head.

They're getting emotional about secondary things, but they're untouched by the fact that Jesus' life is in danger at this point in time.

I know plenty of Christians, men in particular, who never get emotional about the gospel, and yet they'll be punching the air or close to tears of despair over their football team's latest results. In the same way, lots of us get more emotional behind our steering wheels than we do in prayer and worship.

Let's be very clear on this: I'm not encouraging you to force out what you do not feel. If you feel numb – be honest about it! Express that numbness to God.

Emotional engagement with your creator cannot be faked – there's no fooling God, who sees right to the heart of each one of us. Your outward emotional behaviour towards God is for an audience of one – the only one that truly counts.

If the men in that room had said, *Jesus, I see this act of adoration and it only makes me realise how numb and penny-pinching I am – help me!'* well, Jesus' response would have been pure compassion for their repentance. He wanted to change their hearts towards God – and he still wants that today; for hard hearts to grow soft towards God.

God wants a Mary-Generation, a movement of men and women who are emotionally alive to him.

But how did Mary find the courage to lay her heart out in the open before others, to worship emotionally regardless of the opposition this would arouse? Where did this emotional response come from? And, if I'm feeling numb, is there any hope for me?

Awakenings

Here's the good news: the source of her right emotional aliveness was from something to which you and I have complete, glorious, free access.

It came from relationship with Christ, a deep awareness of who she was because of him, and a huge sense of gratitude for the life he had restored her to. It's worth noting that this woman's gratitude to

Jesus happens before he is crucified and rises again. How much more thankful can we be, living post-resurrection in the knowledge of all that God has done to restore us to right relationship with him?

Oswald Chambers, the 19th Century Scottish evangelist, said, *"All heaven is interested in the cross of Christ, all hell terribly afraid of it, while men are the only beings who more or less ignore its meaning."*

God going to the cross and dying for the sins of you and me is not something that it is appropriate for us to be indifferent to. It's something that God wants to unlock emotion in us about because, as we really understand what God did and why it suddenly means so much more to us, everything else pales into insignificance and our priorities realign themselves.

Romans 8:32 says, *'He who did not spare his own Son but gave him up for us all, how will he not also with him graciously give us all things?'*

This needs to sink into our being and become personal. So many of us can't remember the last time that we were really deeply moved emotionally by the difference that Christ brings to us – in our identity, value, purpose and our future, and, most significantly, through his death on the cross – and all because of love. God doesn't want us to stay in that place of numb response.

Christ's death and resurrection has set you free – just as this woman had received life that was precious through Christ, so have you.

Press PAUSE ⑪

How are you doing on this? If you're identifying feeling emotionally dead or detached in your response to Christ, take hold of yourself today, and take heart: there's hope.

I heard recently of an 85-year-old woman who become a

Christian, and she stood up at the church, shaking with nerves, to give her testimony, and she said, *"I suddenly realised that Jesus took my sin away, and I'm 85, so there must have been loads of it!"* I need to be aware of just how much I've been forgiven: *everything!* And I must let the cost of that forgiveness sink in.

At the same time, God doesn't want me to be ruled by over-sensitivity, a raging mass of constant manic outpouring.

My kids have some little wind-up toys, clockwork cars and animals; you wind them up and off they go, and then they flip and spin off in different directions.

That's how I can be when I'm ruled by my emotions. They carry me along one way, and then suddenly spin me off in the other direction.

Just recently I was driving into a Christian event and ahead of me one of my best friends was being directed into a VIP parking spot. When they'd moved off, the car parking steward flatly pointed us to the 'Far car park, please': the one miles away from the building. Who cares, right? Absolutely. I didn't. But then I did. The little voice appeared and suddenly a friend became an emeny.

Later that week, the same guy chirpily commented that someone had anonymously given him a £200 gift token. Great! *So* thrilled! And I *was*. And then I wasn't. *No one's done that for you, Tom...*

Envy steals; it robs; it strips bare. It makes ugly someone and something that was previously beautiful. Although its voice seems so alluring, it is actually a killer. It drags down, mercilessly derailing person after person.

In his book, *The Emotionally Healthy Church*, Peter L. Scazarro describes people who appear 'spiritually mature', but whose emotional state paints a different picture of what's going on inside:

"The church leader who never says, 'I was wrong' or, 'Sorry'. The children's church leader who constantly criticises others. The high control small group leader, who cannot tolerate different points of view. The 35-year-old husband, busily serving in the church, unaware of his wife's loneliness at home. The worship leader who interprets any suggestion as a personal attack and personal rejection. The Sunday School leader struggling with feelings of bitterness and resentment towards the pastor, but afraid to say anything. The two pray-ers who use prayer meetings to escape from the painful reality of their marriage..."

So near, yet so far.

Hallelujah, our God wants to help us! He doesn't dessert us in our plight. So what is the answer? How do I take hold of my emotions?

Will and Grace

Mary felt adoration for Jesus – and so, as a natural consequence of that feeling, she acted.

When you fall in love with someone, you find yourself *doing* something to show that person how you feel. You can't just sit still and *think* about the feelings welling up inside you. Deep love, admiration and respect for another inspires *action*: it must be communicated.

However, let's be real here. There is no getting away from our nature: as human beings, when we have been in a relationship for a while, we have a terrible, shameful propensity for apathy – taking our loved one for granted and failing to express the very adoration that brought us into that relationship in the first place.

So it can be with our relationship with Christ: our human nature, with its preference for comfort and ease, tempts us to forget our passion and obey our physical desires instead and to fear the criticism and judgement of those around us if we appear vulnerable and extravagant in our worship of Christ. Also, we complicate our motives and confuse ourselves in the process: *Am I doing this for God, or to look good in front of others?* Once we start thinking like this, we freeze up, stuck between self-consciousness, pride and self-doubt. We have missed the moment.

Interestingly, the response in marriage vows, before a couple set out on a relationship that requires continual emotional engagement and vulnerability, can offer us some insight here. Couples embarking on this journey of faith when asked if they will love the other person for as long as they both shall live, respond not, *'I do'*, as is often portrayed in the movies, but with the declaration, *'I will.'*

Just as in a marriage, in our relationship with Christ we cannot rely on a feeling to trigger an emotional response. Our commitment to Jesus only deepens if we 'will' it: God gives us free choice, and that free choice comes fresh to us on a daily basis, even a minute-by-minute basis: to pursue him, heart and soul, to engage our minds and meditate on his great act of love and liberty for us, or to turn away.

We have a choice – we *will* or we won't. When I talk about our will, I don't mean we must have will-power: we can do nothing in our own power. Instead, we must draw on another, supernatural power to aid us when our comfort-loving humanity gets the better of us.

Check Your Reality

Use this space to journal your thoughts:
What in your life stirs your emotions?

_____

_____

_____

_____

When did you last cry, and what was it that made you cry?

_____

_____

_____

_____

_____

How hard / easy do you find it to respond emotionally in all the different areas of your life?

_____

_____

_____

_____

_____

Try it Yourself...

❖ Pray that God will give you specific applications for this message. Ask him to awake your soul, your heart, and your emotions to him afresh. Ask him to remove any numbness you feel, and to touch your heart right now. Ask him to bring to mind something you've read in this chapter, and to show you what it is he wants to reveal to you about himself today.

❖ Meditate on scripture, let the words of Jesus fill your soul. Write out portions of scripture - make artwork, bookmarks, paint them on mugs or tiles - hang your artwork up in your kitchen, loo, bedroom... be really practical about getting God's word into your daily life.

Take It Further

Recommended reading:

The Emotionally Healthy Church by Peter Scazarro

Short Christians by Liz Jennings

Chapter Eight

One Almighty Wake Up Call

Mark 14:32–42

This next story in Mark helps us to understand more deeply the need for us to engage and battle with our innate apathy in order to live the relationship with him that God longs for us to experience. Let us join the disciples and Jesus again, this time in the Garden of Gethsemane.

'And they went to a place called Gethsemane. And he said to his disciples, "Sit here while I pray." And he took with him Peter and James and John, and began to be greatly distressed and troubled. And he said to them, "My soul is very sorrowful, even to death. Remain here and watch." And going a little farther, he fell on the ground and prayed that, if it were possible, the hour might pass from him.'

Remember, Jesus came to earth as a fully human being. Just like you and me. Physical pain was to him as it is to us. He knows he's going to face death in a terrible way, and he's also facing taking the sins of the *entire* world with him – he's walking toward an ordeal beyond any terror you or I can imagine. His emotions are real, his soul is troubled, indeed, he's in such a state that he's sweating blood; but look at his prayer in verse 36:

"Abba, Father, all things are possible for you. Remove this cup from me. Yet, not what I will, but what you will." And then he came and found them sleeping, and he said to Peter, "Simon, are you asleep? Could you not watch one hour? Watch and pray that you may not enter into temptation…"

His will is kicking in and governing his emotions. He carries on in verses 38-42:

"…The spirit indeed is willing, but the flesh is weak." And again he went away and prayed, saying the same words. And again he came and found them sleeping, for their eyes were very heavy, and they did not know what to answer him. And he came the third time and said to them "Are you still sleeping and taking your rest? It is enough; the hour has come. The Son of Man is betrayed into the hands of sinners. Rise, let us be going; see, my betrayer is at hand."

Jesus' will is winning through, he is razor-sharp, and spiritually alert to the immensity of what's happened. His disciples, who have a unique moment in history to partner with God, couldn't have got any nearer - and yet they couldn't have been further away. And it was because they weren't *engaging* their wills.

Remember, when we talk about the will, we mean that ability that God has given all of us to *make* choices. It's that ability to listen to my emotions, but to ultimately give those emotions to Jesus and ask his help in making decisions despite how I might be feeling. It's the difference that Jesus describes between the willing spirit and the weak flesh. This battle rages in every single human heart between the part of me that responds to God, and that part of me that thinks £25,000 of perfume poured upon Jesus' head is an extravagant waste of money and that staying awake to pray when I'm tired is too hard. The bible tells me that, when I became a Christian, the power of sin me was broken, but the presence of sin still remains in my life and in the world. I am a new creation, but I have to understand that my 'flesh' - that sinful part of me that prefers comfort to trouble and cares more about my own desires and reputation than about what Jesus desires or what others think of him - still exists in me. If I think that there is no sin in me, i.e. I'm perfect, then I'm completely deluded and I'll be horrendously ineffective for God.

This story could have been so different! It could have gone: *'...And the eleven pushed through their tiredness, they prayed like never before, and Jesus was greatly encouraged.'*

The disciples were obviously physically tired, and, let's face it, we've all been there. But physical tiredness is not really the problem that is being highlighted to me as I read this passage.

The problem I sense is spiritual lethargy: apathy. The disciples have failed to grasp the desperate urgency of this moment, and the importance of their prayers to Jesus.

Sleepy Christians

I can be such a sleepy Christian! Do you ever feel that you're snoozing through your Christian life?

2 Corinthians 10: 5b tells us we are to take every thought captive. We're called to be those who aren't just led by our emotions (which can switch and change from moment to moment) but to be

exercising our will over our emotions; to be aware of them, capturing them, examining them before God and deciding whether to keep them captive or let them go free.

And our *will* - that God-given ability to choose what we *do* about what we feel - is profoundly important, because we are in a battle. The Christian life is always a fight, it's not peace-time until Jesus has returned and ended the battle. If I am governed by my emotions, I will give in to them.

A friend of mine, Dave King, leads a church in Tunbridge Wells. I was speaking to him about his church's new building, and I asked if he'd got really excited about it. He told me, '*I love people and I don't get so excited about buildings, so I thought, "It's fairly interesting, it's a building... fine." But I realised, a few months in, that Satan was anything but asleep over this project. He was on red alert. He understood the significance of a church getting a long-term physical presence in a place. I suddenly saw all the opposition, and things that started happening within the church, and it was like a wake-up call.*'

I love this quote from A. J. Gossip, professor of Christian Ethics and Practical Theology at the University of Glasgow from 1939-1945:

"You will not stroll into Christ-likeness with your hands in your pockets, shoving the door open with a careless shoulder. This isn't a hobby for one's leisure moments, taken up at intervals when we have nothing much to do, and put down and forgotten when our life grows full and interesting. It takes all of one's strength, one's heart, one's mind, and soul."

So, how do I grow into Christ-likeness? And does God's grace extend to the mountain of apathy, unwillingness and cynicism that so often fights for control of my heart?

The Cure

The good news, my friend, is that God's cure for us is simple. Firstly, knowing the gospel of the cross and remaining mindful of it keeps us emotional about God. Remembering the chains that Christ has broken for us and the old life he has set us free from keeps our hearts thankful. Knowing our identity as God's child keeps us joyful. And then, the gospel of the Spirit provides us with the cure for spiritual sleepiness.

Romans 8:13 crystallises it beautifully.

'For if you live according to the flesh you will die, but if by the Spirit you put to death the deeds of the body, you will live.'

It's not about how hard I try. Something has to shift in my thinking that is far more profound than human effort. My will alone is not going to be enough for me to actually do the will of God and overcome my emotions.

Thankfully for all of us, after the day of Pentecost, when the Holy Spirit was poured out, everything changed. It's like our human will – or *'spirit'* with a small *'s'*, gets supercharged by the Holy Spirit, huge great big capital *'S'*.

My attempts in my human strength to do the right thing suddenly get dwarfed by a huge *'S'*, the person of Jesus Christ in the Holy Spirit. I suddenly realise that the reason that Jesus was able in this moment to do what was beyond his capabilities to cope with as a man was because he was filled and flooded with the person of the Holy Spirit, capital *'S'*. At Pentecost the Holy Spirit got poured out for *all* believers. It means that when my little *'s'* thinks, *'I should do the right thing,'* along comes Mr Big *'S'* to say, *'You can do it - with MY power!'*

The same power that raised Christ from the dead is in us! I'll say that again: The same power that raised Christ from the dead is *in you and me*! SO, WHAT CAN'T WE DO?! The power is not ours — there's no self-belief in this message. The power is God's.

One of the biggest battles as a Christian is knowing who I am in Christ already. It's not about knowing who I could be if I really try hard and pray loads. If you are a Christian, you are someone who has the big 'S' of the Holy Spirit in you, which means the small 's' — your own spirit of desire to do the right thing and overcome your emotions - has been supercharged like never before.

When my human will wants — or doesn't want - to do something, I can just say *Hallelujah!* Because the Holy Spirit is towering over whatever it is, ready to empower me. This means that I can overcome my emotions by the power of the Holy Spirit, day by day, hour by hour, moment by moment.

Its application is so down-to-earth: its daily effect in my life is direct.

Now, I like snowboarding, I like sleeping, I like no responsibility. Ah, simple pleasures! The idea of me having a time with God in the morning when I could be sleeping, is emotionally the least attractive thing on planet earth to me.

Yet, in the midst of my free-and-easy preferences, I yearn to communicate God's love with my kids, and I recognise that breakfast with them is a precious moment to do this. It's a tiny window before they go out into the world of school and various groups and have information pumped into them. They're going to be given stories, fairy tales, and all sorts of stuff all day long; some of it will help them, and some of it will harm them. But, for this one moment, they're all mine, and I have a God-given opportunity.

Of course, I'd rather just eat my bran flakes. My emotions are very clear on the subject. I need the Holy Spirit to govern my will.

Practically, it means I need to go to bed earlier than I, emotionally, would like to. And, believe me, when my alarm goes off early in the morning, every part of my *emotional* being just wants to stay asleep. It's only asking the Holy Spirit to supercharge my will that gets me downstairs to splash water in my face. I set a little timer on the heater in my shed so that when I walk in there's a wave of heat, and I get in that shed with a cup of tea, and I feel like a snail first thing in the morning. I have to read everything again and again because my brain isn't firing up yet, and I'm desperately trying to get going.

But I realised quickly in my walk with God that, if I don't do that, no one else will do it for me. I use that time to read the bible and thank God for whatever I'm reading and for what it teaches me about him.

I go in feeling fearful every day: overwhelmed, intimidated and despairing at times. Your elders, pastors, vicars, rectors, bishops and every other Christian leader you can think of feel those sorts of emotions every day. Christianity is a very level playing field.

My Spirit-dependent-will drags me in there, kicking and screaming, and I say, *"God, please help me!"*

There's no burst of light, but bit by bit, through reading the bible and thanking God, I start to wake up afresh. My emotions get newly aligned with who God is and who I am. And so, at 7.30, desperate for the bran flakes, I'm ready to go for it with my kids, getting that bible story read and communicating something of God's love for them.

Let me say with all my heart, I don't want to be legalistic about this and turn it into a set of rules to follow. We don't sit there like The Waltons in perfect peace and pious harmony. Our lives are as messy as everyone else's, with pressures and worries and to-do lists and every human emotion under the sun. It's not a scientific formula, but experience has taught me that if I want to stay spiritually alert so that I know what's going on in my emotions, and am able to keep on track so that I can be used for Christ in my life, I have to be someone who calls upon the super '*S*' Holy Spirit to overcome and use my will to enable me to do the things my emotions would never enable me to do. I need to engage my emotions, but I cannot rely upon them.

C.S. Lewis said, *'I end most days feeling pretty good, and then I wake up in the morning, and I feel like a skin of sin has grown over me.'* I so identify with that. I wake up every morning, and I'm back to square one: Lord, here I am. *Help me again to know that it's not all about me, but it's all about you.*

Press PAUSE ⑪

How are you doing with this? Are you consciously inviting the Holy Spirit to supercharge your will? Are you pushing deeper into Christ in ways that demand supernatural strength? If you can 'do' Christianity in your own strength without ever having to cry out to God to get you through a day, then I'm sorry to say it sounds like you've found 'Religion' rather than a relationship with your maker.

It should encourage us to know that we have the same power in us that Jesus had. It's not just a vague thing: we really do. It will be different for all of us, and we each have to figure it out our own way. But nobody else can do it for us.

Don't let it be true in your life that you were someone who came to church, listened, nodded, amen-ed, but never actually allowed yourself to *feel* anything, to have an emotional response to the message of Jesus Christ. At the same time, don't let yourself be ruled by your emotions: engage the will God has given you, once again holding each emotional response openly to him for his guidance. Don't let apathy cause you to take your relationship with God for granted.

The Spirit is with you, and *will* help you.

Check Your Reality

Use this space to journal your thoughts:

What areas of your life do you need the Holy Spirit's help in to practically live out your faith in the face of fear or apathy?

_____

_____

_____

_____

How could you introduce time alone with God and his word to the rhythm of your daily life?

_____

_____

_____

_____

Try it Yourself...

❖ Be creative in connecting with God: get out some paints and paper and pray as your draw or paint. Don't limit God to a five minute 'quiet time' - seek new ways to connect and worship.

❖ Go for a run - sing worship songs as you run, thank God and listen for his prompting: you're running with the Spirit!

❖ Remember - this is not about dragging Jesus into our daily lives: he's already here. It's about acknowledging his presence and aligning ourselves with the Holy Spirit's leading - and as we make space in our lives for him, we'll find depths of intimacy beyond our imaginings!

Take It Further

Recommended reading:

Disruptive Discipleship: The Power of Breaking Routine to Kickstart Your Faith by Sam van Eman, Inter Varsity Press

If You Want To Walk On Water You've Got To Get Out Of The Boat by John Ortberg, Zondervan publications

Chapter Nine

Mark 14:53–54; 66–68

Between a Rock and a Hard Place

As the religious and political temperature around Jesus reaches fever pitch, we've observed the reactions of those closest to him. What scripture shows us is that his friends and followers went through emotions and physical states that we can completely relate to as part of our human brokenness. What we've also seen is that, regardless of how disappointed, frustrated or hurt Jesus must have felt by those around him, he remained obedient to the will of God. And so we come to the next section of Mark, and things are about to get really tough for one disciple in particular.

'And they led Jesus to the high priest. All the chief priests and the elders and the scribes came together. And Peter had followed him at a distance, right into the

courtyard of the high priest. And he was sitting with the guards and warming himself at the fire...'

These verses in Mark talk not about the emotions or the will, but about actions. That moment when our character reveals itself through what we do.

We see Jesus (the true 'rock') standing before the Scribes and the Elders and looking them in the eye, saying words that will condemn him to death, and we see Peter, whom Jesus has nicknamed 'The Rock', behaving in a rather un-rock-like way to say the least.

We can only imagine what's going through each figure's mind: Jesus is steadfastly continuing on the path God has placed before him. As he stands there, he's confronted with lie after lie, the people he came to serve turning on him for their moment of glory, hoping to somehow profit by his death. Once again, the religious leaders of the day lead the persecution of the son of the God they claim to serve, unable to reconcile him to their rule-book in his non-conformity: God was not who they expected, and they were not willing to consider the possibility of their having made a mistake. And where are his followers? The men and women who've devoted themselves to him until this point don't even feature – and we'll look more at this in the next chapter. Our focus now is on Peter's story, and it's rich with lessons for us.

Christ stands, abandoned, despised, maligned and yet steadfast. Here is our God! Unshakable, unbreakable; he'll never let us down. In contrast, while Jesus faces execution, Peter's emotions, will and actions are all over the place in verses 66-68.

'And as Peter was below in the courtyard, one of the servant girls of the high priest came, and seeing Peter warming himself, she looked at him and said, "You were also with the Nazarene, Jesus." But he denied it, saying, "I neither know nor understand what you mean."'

The evening began with Jesus and the disciples together in a party mood, them exuberantly professing their loyalty to him, declaring, *'We will follow you anywhere, Jesus...'* Now here we are, a few hours later: Jesus is alone, condemned to death and his closest friends are denying they ever knew him.

One of my faith heroes is J. C. Ryle. In 1880, at age 64, he became the first Anglican bishop of Liverpool. He remained true to the bible at a time when the church as a whole had turned its back on the authority of scripture. That meant that he was hated, a little bit like Jesus was hated.

Year upon year, he would not stop proclaiming the word of God. He was described as something of a giant, because of both his great height, and his great courage. He said, *"There's an epidemic going on now, especially among young Christians. And it produces what I must venture to call a 'jellyfish Christianity'. Christianity without bone, muscle or power."*

Today, we have hundreds of 'jellyfish' church leaders, and thousands of 'jellyfish' sermons preached every year without a single bone, no definite opinion to be found. Worst of all, we have thousands of 'jellyfish' worshippers, respectable church-going people who have no distinct, definite views about anything to do with God.

Press PAUSE ⑪

How are you doing on this? Giant, or jellyfish?

Peter went into this moment feeling like a giant: *'If I must die with you, I will not deny you.'* (v31). When the moment came, he turned to jelly.

How do we learn from Peter's experience? The stakes are high: God has positioned you in your workplace, with your neighbours, in your family, with your housemates, in your lecture halls and your seminars - and your life is just as significant as Peter's, just as significant as J.C. Ryle's, just as significant as C.S. Lewis. You're here today because God has got a specific plan for you, and you're going to face giant-or-jellyfish moments throughout your life.

It's worth spending a few minutes considering Peter's story. We've been given it for a reason, and there's an opportunity here of deepening our knowledge of and love for Christ: let's take it now.

The Timing Of Your Life

The key to Peter's behaviour is all in the timing. At this point, he's got to know Jesus pretty well. He's witnessed many miracles happen before his eyes, from feeding thousands of people from a single lunchbox to walking on water. He's got close to Jesus, emotionally as well as physically. He's left family to be a disciple. He really believes in the things Jesus has told him. He's passionately devoted to this man and wants part of this new kingdom that Jesus is releasing on earth.

What's hard for us to really appreciate is how, at this moment, Peter doesn't know how the story ends. All he knows is that everything he thought was solid is evaporating in front of him, and it looks like his life is in danger. He doesn't know about the Happy Ever After that is to come when Jesus returns having beaten death. He must be absolutely terrified at this point.

From Here to Eternity

What is so glorious and wonderful is that although Peter fails, in this moment, for all the world to know forever in scripture, it isn't the end of his story. Peter, the jellyfish in this moment, ends his life as Peter the giant for Christ. It's partly because of the Spirit coming on him, but it's also because of his understanding of the gospel of the resurrection of Jesus Christ.

In 1 Peter 3:17, he says, *'It is better to suffer for doing good, if that should be God's will, than for doing evil.'* That's a giant talking; that's a rock; that's a man who is learning to follow in his master's footsteps.

He lived in the certainty of the gospel that Jesus Christ defeated sin and death and is more alive now than ever. This same Jesus is with you right now, by his Spirit, loving you, watching you, urging you on; he's *for* you, and he watches every element of your life. And that's meant to be the most amazing encouragement, and also just a little bit scary because this is God we're talking about.

It has to be like that because otherwise the fears of this life will overwhelm us: *'Telling that person about Christ? That's scary!'* But you need to know that when you're doing these things, God is with you.

Oswald Chambers said, *"The remarkable thing about God is that when you fear God, you fear nothing else whereas if you do not fear God, you fear everything else."*

There's that bit in *The Chronicles of Narnia*, where it says about Aslan, the lion, *'Is he safe? No, but he's good.'*

Jesus Christ isn't safe, and following him is not a retreat into a cosy haven.

C.S. Lewis said, *"I didn't go to religion to make me happy. I always knew a bottle of port would do that. If you want a religion to make you feel really comfortable, I certainly don't recommend Christianity."*

I must live every day in the certainty that Christ is with me, right now. And when I live like that, I can embrace the adventure of life with God through the Holy Spirit.

The Key to Your Heart

Imagine the potential of a church who are governing their emotions, using their wills, and then their actions, so that, on Monday morning, all over the nation, God has opportunities to show himself. Imagine an army of people living with that sense of the gospel of the raised and returning Christ. That would change the world!

My heart must be stirred by the gospel of the cross; my will must be alert to the gospel of the Spirit, and I need the courage that comes from God, knowing that he is with me every single step of the way, and he will return.

This is one of the greatest themes in the New Testament, it was how they were able to do what they did, because they knew that Jesus Christ was raised and he was going to return. They didn't just live as if this life was everything, they lived the complete opposite! There are men and women on this planet living like that right now, and they are seeing God work in the most incredible ways.

God's desire is to raise up a church that would be fearless. He doesn't want me to be living for approval, and the things that so grip this world. He wants to wake us in these days. He wants our lives to change. Can you sense the mood in the nation changing? Day, by day, by day, in some ways greater favour, in some ways, greater persecution. The smile of opportunities opening up, while, simultaneously, hostility grows.

We may be on the side of the good guy, but heroes have enemies. This is where our relationship with Christ plays its part: we need to know exactly who he is, and it's that heart knowledge of him that changes everything.

You and I have *one chance* to live this life for Christ: one chance! We must battle daily to engage with Christ, his death and resurrection, in a way that affects our feelings, thoughts, words and deeds. We're not in a religion, we're in a relationship, and we need to get to know our God intimately.

Check Your Reality

Use this space to journal your thoughts:
What has Christ set you free from? What chains has his death and resurrection broken in your life?

_____

_____

_____

_____

Take this opportunity to write a prayer for the church here, that we would be the bringer of God's kingdom as he longs for us to be.

_____

_____

_____

_____

Try it Yourself...

❖ Go for a thankful walk or run – whichever floats your boat. Spend between ten and thirty minutes walking or running and thanking Jesus for the difference he's made in your life. You might struggle to begin, but once you start, more thank-yous will flow. Be really practical about it – thank God for the shoes on your feet as well as the salvation of the cross.

Take It Further

Recommended reading:

The Jesus I Never Knew by Philip Yancey

What's So Amazing About Grace by Philip Yancey

Chapter Ten

Mark 14:53-65; Mark 15:1-10

Missing the Messiah

We remain at the trial, but shift our focus as Mark's gospel shows us Jesus getting an audience with the religious leaders of his day. These men were the ecclesiastical crème-de-la-crème; the aristocracy of the priesthood. They knew their bibles like nobody else. They could quote great chunks of the Old Testament verbatim. They could pray harder and longer than anybody else. They gave huge amounts of money to the temple on a regular basis. In short, these guys had serious religious credentials.

And yet, with Jesus standing before them, they don't recognise him for who he is. Despite knowing the Old Testament and its many references and prophecies about Jesus, they manage to completely miss the Messiah standing right there in the room.

'...And they led Jesus to the high priest. And all the chief priests and the elders and the scribes came together. And Peter had followed him at a distance, right into the courtyard of the high priest. And he was sitting with the guards and warming himself at the fire. Now the chief priests and the whole council were seeking testimony against Jesus to put him to death, but they found none. For many bore false witness against him, but their testimony did not agree. And some stood up and bore false witness against him, saying, "We heard him say, 'I will destroy this temple that is made with hands, and in three days I will build another not made with hands.'" Yet even about this their testimony did not agree. And the high priest stood up in the midst and asked Jesus, "Have you no answer to make? What is it that these men testify against you?" But he remained silent and made no answer. Again, the high priest asked him, "Are you the Christ, the Son of the Blessed?" And Jesus said, "I am, and you will see the Son of Man seated at the right hand of Power, and coming with the clouds of heaven." And the high priest tore his garments and said, "What further witnesses do we need? You have heard his blasphemy. What is your decision?" And they all condemned him as deserving death. And some began to spit on him and to cover his face and to strike him, saying to him, "Prophesy!" And the guards received him with blows.'

Rough Justice

You don't have to be Sherlock Holmes to deduce that this is a dodgy trial. It's a total shambles of mismatched lies and conceit. And then the high priest, the leader of God's people, Israel, the religious leader of all the chief priests and the scribes, approaches Jesus, and asks him straight: *"Have you no answer to make? What is it that these men testify against you?"*

When Jesus just looks back at him saying nothing, this would have rubbed the high priest up the wrong way. The high priest was considered by all, including himself, to be the most important person in the room, subordinate only to Pilate, the Roman Emperor.

Jesus likes us to work him out for ourselves: I can be told who Jesus is by someone else, but it's only when I engage with him myself on a personal level, piecing together all that I know, sense and understand, that things shift within me. It's when I search my own heart as I gaze at him, that I'm able to see him in all his glory and humility, holiness and humanity.

The high priest misses his chance. Infuriated by Jesus' lack of response, he demands an answer: *"Are you the Christ? Are you the Son of the blessed?"*

This man would have been aware of the last three years of Jesus' ministry, of the things he'd been saying, of the lives he'd changed, of the healings, the miracles, the raising of the dead.

Lots of atheists will gladly say that Jesus was a good man who never claimed to be God: this verse is for them. As the chief priest desperately tries to intimidate the Son of God, he backs himself into the corner he dreads, the corner that threatens everything he and his colleagues have built for themselves over generations.

Jesus answers him, *"I am."*

It's the answer that turns the world upside down for the high priest. And Jesus follows it with an illustration from the Old Testament book, Daniel, where he talks about the Son of Man being lifted up, and given dominion over the earth by God himself.

The Jewish understanding of that passage was that the 'Son of Man' spoken about in Daniel was Israel: God's people. The high priest and his colleagues believed that in this text, the Son of Man was actually *them*, and that God was going to lift *them* up, and show that they were in the right and *everybody* else was wrong.

Jesus takes that passage and explains it in a way that turns their version of God upside down, and destroys their vision of personal glory for the future.

It doesn't go down well. Have you ever tried ripping your garments? It's not easy to do: you've got to be in quite a state of fury to manage something like that. I can imagine the hysterical tone of their voices as they cry, *"Blasphemy!"* and condemn him to death.

Historians don't even think that this is a statement worthy of the cry of blasphemy: Jesus hasn't said anything directly about God: he's said something about *them*. But their understanding of God is so fixed on *who they are*, and their egos are so deeply offended, they're left with only one option if they wish to maintain their power over the people. They must get rid of Jesus, for good.

It's tragic, because they knew their bibles so well; they were the most enthusiastic pray-ers and worshippers, spent all their time hanging out in the temple... translate it into modern day church terms, and you've got the ones at the front; the super-keenies. The ones we all look to and think, *'What great Christians!'*

Well, they're great at 'religion', but they've missed something vital, and it makes me want to scream at them, *"He's right there in front of you! Why can't you see it?"*

Motivation For Murder

The reason they miss the Messiah is surprising. It's not due to materialism, fear or unbelief. The reason they're killing Jesus is perceived by the Roman emperor, a man who probably didn't know his bible at all:

'And as soon as it was morning, the chief priests held a consultation with the elders and scribes and the whole council. And they bound Jesus and led him away

and delivered him over to Pilate. And Pilate asked him, "Are you the King of the Jews?" And he answered him "You have said so." And the chief priests accused him of many things. And Pilate again asked him, "Have you no answer to make? See how many charges they bring against you." But Jesus made no further answer, so that Pilate was amazed.

Now at the feast he used to release for them one prisoner for whom they asked. And among the rebels in prison, who had committed murder in the insurrection, there was a man called Barabbas. And the crowd came up and began to ask Pilate to do as he usually did for them. And he answered them, saying, "Do you want me to release for you the King of the Jews?" For he perceived that it was out of envy that the chief priests had delivered him up.'

It's all about envy!

A really helpful way of understanding envy is to offset it against jealousy.

Jealousy can be understood as when you want something, when you are fiercely protective over something which is, actually, by rights, yours. If you're engaged, and somebody starts making moves on your fiancé, putting their arm around them in front of you, giving them an uninvited kiss and taking them out on dates - your anger will be a jealous one, and that would be fair enough.

Envy is different. Envy is when you want something you have no right to, and the idea of somebody else having it drives you mad: it makes you hate them. We're all susceptible to envy, no one is immune. It might be that you have great athletic ability, and you pride yourself on a good level of fitness. But how do you feel if your best friend suddenly gets sporty, and they turn out to be an incredible athlete? The attention's on them and their astonishing natural ability. You've been at it for years, but somehow you're suddenly fading into the background.

This is what Pilate saw that the chief priests felt towards Jesus: envy of him. Jesus knew this himself.

Son and Heir

Several chapters earlier in Mark 12:1-8, Jesus tells the story - a parable - of the tenants, and the story goes like this.

"A man planted a vineyard and put a fence around it and dug a pit for the winepress and built a tower, and leased it to tenants and went into another country. When the season came, he sent a servant to the tenants to get from them some of the fruit of the vineyard. And they took him and beat him and sent him away empty-handed. Again he sent to them another servant, and they struck him on the head and treated him shamefully. And he sent another, and him they killed. And so with many others: some they beat, and some they killed. He had still one other, a beloved son. Finally he sent him to them, saying, 'They will respect my son.' But those tenants said to one another, 'This is the heir. Come, let us kill him, and the inheritance will be ours.' And they took him and killed him and threw him out of the vineyard."

Jesus is the Son of God. He comes into God's creation as its heir. He is the centre of it, not the chief priests. This is the clincher for them. They think that they are the centre of God's purposes. This is why they love to pray, because it's all about them looking really holy and impressive. This is why they love to study and memorise the bible, because it makes them feel clever and superior. They love to give because they like to look rich and generous, and also pious and holy.

They think God is all about them, and when Jesus tells them otherwise, they hate him for it, and reject him.

Ironically, it's in this very rejection that they give the game up. In Luke 10:16, Jesus said, *"...the one who rejects me rejects him who sent me."* In showing that they don't recognise the Messiah, they reveal that they don't even know God.

Green-Eyed Monsters

The bible says, ultimately, that we are envious of God. Now, that's probably not something I feel aware of guilt over generally. I might confess to feeling envy over a friend's lifestyle or possessions, but you're not likely to see me sitting with a friend over a coffee and saying *"Yeah, I'm really struggling with feeling envious of God right now."* It sounds a bit bonkers, doesn't it?

But when you bear in mind a definition of envy as me wanting something that I have no right to it begins to make sense because God is at the centre of the universe - he's the one who has the right to say what it should look like, how it should be - and that's the exact temptation I face.

Richard Dawkins is one of the most vocal atheists of our day, and in his book *The God Delusion*, he writes:

"Jesus was not content to derive his ethics from the scriptures of his upbringing. He explicitly departed from them... Since a principle thesis of this chapter is that we do not, and should not, derive our morals from scriptures, Jesus has to be honoured as a model for that very thesis..."

What an interesting thought process! It's an acknowledgement of Jesus as a role model, within a simultaneous rejection of his claim to be the Messiah and inheritor of the earth. Like those chief priests of Jesus' day, the idea that there's a God in heaven who can't be controlled or defined by us, but to whom we are accountable and must submit, is deeply offensive.

Perhaps it's hurtful, too. Those chief priests were Important People, and yet, when God came to earth he hung out with prostitutes, swindlers and lepers, rather than spending his time bolstering their egos, confirming their status as those whose knowledge was power.

For such a threatening God, there is only one course of action: to get rid of him.

Press PAUSE ⏸

How are you doing on this?

If you're reading this and you're not a Christian, just humour me for a moment; put aside all arguments for and against God just for a minute, and consider this question: do you really just *not want* God in your life?

As a Christian, I need to take a long hard look at the envy of these scribes and priests. They're so close to Jesus, and yet a million miles away from him. I need to ask myself, how does envy work itself out in my life? Because, uncomfortable though it makes me feel, I'm not immune to envy: one of the things the bible does is it holds a mirror up to us, and enables us to examine our own hearts.

I remember sitting on my bed in my university halls not long after I became a Christian. I was reading the New Testament and finding it a challenge to the way I was living. In a fit of fury, I took my bible and lobbed it at the wall opposite me. I'm not sure what I was trying to achieve by my 'mighty act' of rebellion, but that was my reaction - my emotional response - to the words of Jesus. The gospel offends a selfish lifestyle with its ultimate deposing of me as self-appointed king of my world and its enthroning of the God-anointed King Jesus.

Rivalries and Comparisons

This is how our envy of God works itself out in our envy of other people: the two correlate. *I* want to be the centre, eg, *I want to be God.* When other people are getting what we want, we can resent them. It starts in the heart, and it is so destructive and ugly in church, where we're meant to be a family with God at the centre, cheering each other on as we discover more of his glory and love for us together.

I have to keep checking myself: does the idea of somebody in my small group getting the opportunity to do some leadership bug me? Do I find myself wanting to put them down? Am I hyper-critical of everything they do? Do I struggle with the idea of others being successful in areas of life – both inside church and out – that I would like to be involved in?

This is envy, and it's right in here when the false witnesses lie about Jesus: they're putting him down, trying to find ways to condemn him.

God-Binding

If God is at the centre of the universe and he gets to orchestrate and run it as he pleases, and I'm struggling with the idea that I'm not, my envy works itself out in frustration when I don't get what I want.

And so I say, *'God, why haven't you given me that well paid and influential post at work yet?'* or, *'God, why haven't I got a wife/ husband yet?'* My reactions become angry towards God, because I feel he owes me something.

And it's not about whether they are good things for me to have and enjoy or not. The issue is whether I am content to let God be God whilst I don't have those things. So maybe I test God, and start

171

doing deals with him on my own terms. I say, *"Ok, I'll give to the church building fund as long as I get a pay rise come September."* Or, *"Sure, I'll give up a year of my life as long as by the end of it I've got myself a girlfriend."*

The final destination of that kind of thinking is seen in Mark 15:32, when they crucify Jesus and say, *"Let the Christ, the King of Israel, come down now from the cross that we may see and believe."*

Caught In A Trap

No one's immune to envy, but what those in the grip of envy fail to see is how foolish it makes us.

The chief priests and religious leaders think that by killing Jesus, they can prove him wrong and return the status quo, with themselves back at the centre of it all. Their intention must be to go on living life as before, with God being all about them. And they genuinely seem to think they're proving him wrong and proving themselves right.

Within the darkness of this scene - Jesus on the cross, having been tortured and mocked - we see the surprising victory of Jesus and the good news of Christianity and the gospel. They think they've proved that he's not the Messiah; ironically, they've just enthroned him as Messiah through their own actions.

Unexpectedly, at this point in the story, somebody sees what's really happening here. Mark 15:37-39:

'And Jesus uttered a loud cry and breathed his last. And the curtain of the temple was torn in two, from top to bottom. And when the centurion, who stood facing him, saw that in this way he breathed his last, he said, "Truly this man was the Son of God!"'

This centurion is the total opposite of the chief priests and the scribes. Where they're religious and squeaky clean, he is a rough Roman soldier. Roman soldiers were tough guys: he would have killed and tortured people. And this unlikely man sees Jesus, and he says, *"Truly, this man was the Son of God."*

How did this guy figure that out? Is it that his theology all fell into place suddenly? No. Once again, God turns our wisdom on its head. As long as you know God, he will always surprise you with his ways - they are so often the opposite of the way I would organise the world.

In the ancient world, sons inherited all that their fathers had, taking over their father's business and the responsibility that entailed. Somehow, this centurion, seeing Jesus on the cross, recognises that this man has taken responsibility for God's creation: that he's the heir.

In that moment, on the cross, Jesus paid the cost of our envy of God, and of one another, and of all the evil which stems from that. And this victory of Jesus, it's not just that forgiveness, but it's our freedom, our healing, it's our salvation, it's a way for us to be freed from our envious ways.

I can know as much of the bible as I want, I can read all the Christian books in the world, I can spend hours on my knees praying, I can be at every church meeting I can get myself to - but if I miss the love of God in Jesus, I'm a million miles away from him: I'm still trapped in my envy.

But if, like the centurion, I see it, it doesn't matter how together or otherwise I am, it doesn't matter where I'm at - I've got it: freedom from my sin, forgiveness, healing, salvation, love, hope and finally, wonderfully, I get to become a child of God myself.

We Are Family

I'm no longer just a worshipper in a church or temple: I'm family! A child of the living God, with all the glorious rights of inheritance and love that the children of a perfect father can expect.

And I can know this for sure because of Mark's inclusion of the information that '...*the curtain in the temple was torn in half...*' The temple was where people would find God's presence. But it was very restrictive, because of our sin in contrast with God's holiness, we couldn't come in close and have that experience of a tender, intimate relationship with God. God was there with his people, but he was separate.

Jesus paid the cost for our sin when he died on the cross, and in that moment the curtain that divided the temple, keeping people from God, was torn in half. In this dramatic visual illustration, God breaks out of the temple and he comes to sinners - people like the Roman centurion, and, two thousand years later, me - and he shows us Jesus. He reveals that in Jesus we're saved, we're forgiven, we're restored to that original right relationship that God always intended.

God loves me and I see that in the way that Jesus gave himself up for me. And he loves you too, in just the same crazy, glorious, mind-blowing way. No one is excluded from God's love. No one is too far out of reach. From the high priest to Pilate, from Barabbas to the centurion, God's love is poured out equally, for each person, without prejudice.

It all comes down to my response. If I don't acknowledge him, then that in itself is my answer. But I'll miss a relationship with the most exciting hero the world has ever known.

The choice, because God is gracious beyond my understanding, is mine. It is yours, too, every day. The act, of which no human being is remotely capable, of bridging the void between God and human-kind, is his.

Check Your Reality

Use this space to journal your thoughts:

When do you struggle with envy?

_____

_____

_____

_____

_____

What effects of envy do you see in the world around you?

_____

_____

_____

_____

_____

We saw how Jesus likes us to figure him out for ourselves - do you feel that you've figured him out, or is he a complete mystery to you? Do you think we ever truly figure him out, or does the truth lie somewhere between the two points?

_____

_____

_____

_____

_____

Try it Yourself...

❖ Pray! No surprises there, eh? Seriously, pray about your envy.
  Prayer makes a difference: you can't take your problem to a
  wiser counsellor, or a higher power.

Take It Further

Recommended reading:

The Jesus I Never Knew by Philip Yancey, Zondervan publications

Struggling to be Holy by Judy Hirst, Darton, Longman & Todd Limited
publications

Conclusion

The Comfort Zone

Mark's gospel is intense. The challenge of serious discipleship can be daunting.

But we shouldn't feel overwhelmed: remember - *we are not the hero in this story!* God reaches out to us with open arms of grace every time.

As each challenge rises before us, we have one to whom we can turn, who carries us in a loving embrace. He is the one who has been there before us, who loves us and who is with us for every moment of our lives.

Again and again throughout this book, we've come back to prayer. It is so central! Without prayer, we have no lines of communication to or from God. When we realise how much it cost God to enable us to pray, we begin to get some inkling of how vital it is to God.

If you want to feel a closer communion with God, to be aware of his presence in your life in a moment-by-moment basis, whether you are having a good day or a bad day, then commit to prayer. Spend time in silence; shout; laugh; sing your heart out; cry your eyes out. Only as we face God with utter frailty and dependence upon him, can he work with us and through us.

In Christ, we have the greatest hero the world has ever - or will ever - know. He knows you better than you know yourself, and he loves you more than you could ever imagine. He's *for you*, he's *with you*, and his plans for you really do end in *happy ever after*.

Press PAUSE ⑪

How are you feeling as we come to the end of our time together?

Every day is an opportunity to go deeper with Jesus, to receive more of his grace, to know more of his love for you. But no one can do it for you, and God won't intrude where he's not wanted or invited. Following Christ is the most exciting thing you can do in this life, opening up a surprising supernatural world of mercy and love. Don't miss out on the adventures he has for you!

Check Your Reality:

What sort of Christian experience do you dream of?

_____

_____

_____

_____

_____

Try It Yourself...

❖ Bring the things you have written here to Jesus now and talk them over with him. Spend a few minutes in stillness and silence after you've spoken to give him a chance to respond.

Take It Further

Recommended reading:

No recommendations here, except a prayer from me that you will take your faith further, and in doing so, discover more of the God who loves you and who calls you to a life – and an eternity - with him.

Seek out books that take you deeper into areas of your faith walk that God is drawing you to explore. Don't just buy them online: find them online and then order them in your local bookshop. The last few years have seen a decline in the number of Christian bookshops around the UK, which has been sad to see - but don't miss the opportunity this presents to use our local bookshops as our resource and our market place. Bookshops respond to sales, and the more Christian books they sell, the more they'll stock – and then who knows whose hands they'll fall into, and whose lives they might change?

Remember, our God is the King of creativity. Allow him to lead you on a journey of letting him into every area of your life by offering him access to every part of your life, from car journeys to washing up, from changing nappies to hanging wallpaper, sitting in university lectures to going to your own retirement party. God is speaking to us all the time, and his repeated words to us are, "I love you, I love you,

I love you. I know you intimately and I love you eternally. Don't try and do this life alone! Come and rest in my power. Get to know me. Work *with* me and together we'll have great adventures."

About the Authors

Tom Shaw was born and raised in the UK and has been an active part of the church community since 1997. He became an elder in 2003, married Josie in 2004 and they now have three daughters, Daisy, Lily and Poppy. For ten years, Tom was the lead elder at The City Church in Canterbury, UK and was instrumental in birthing many churches worldwide. Eventually Tom was called to California where he served on staff as Director of Leadership Development at Radiant Church for two years. Tom is planting Sanctuary Church in San Francisco where he enjoys his three loves: curry, coffee and conversation.

Liz Jennings grew up in a South London vicarage in the 1970s, the youngest of three children. At sixteen, she moved with her parents to the Midlands, returning to London two years later to study for an English and Theology degree. She has written features and fiction for a variety of Christian and secular publications, from Tearfund to Take A Break. She met her husband, Mark, while temping in Clapham. They have two children, Maisie and Reuben, and live in Kent, UK. She runs writing groups for people with a diagnosis of dementia and was the editor for *Welcome To Our World*, available from the Alzheimer's Society. Her other books include *Short Christians* and *Blank For Your Own Message*.

You can follow Tom Shaw on Facebook, Instagram and

www.tomshawblog.com

Another Book by Liz Jennings

Short Christians

Exploring Faith Together Through Fiction - a Study Guide for Small Groups.

Short Christians contains twelve short stories that follow the lives of different Christian characters through a particular moment in their faith journeys.

These stories have been created to enable small groups and individuals to reflect, share ideas and find fresh points of connection in a relaxed, enjoyable and stimulating way.

Each story is followed by ideas for discussion, encouragement to listen, points for prayer and space to write reflections. In addition at the end of the book are author notes, which reveal some intriguing insights into the characters and the author's thought process.

"A great tool for small groups to open up honest discussions that go a little deeper!" – Sarah, small group member

Published by Lioness Writing Ltd
www.lionesswritingltd.com
ISBN: 0993438393   ISBN-13: 978-0993438394
6" x 9" (152 x 229 mm)   Paperback: 208 pages
Price: £7.99/$9.99   Released 30 September 2017

Available via Eden (formerly CLC), Gardners, Waterstones, Amazon, or any other good booksellers.

More resources on:

www.lastminutesmallgroup.com